WEST OF WALL STREET

WEST OF WALL STREET

George Angell
Barry Haigh

 Longman Financial Services Publishing
a division of Longman Financial Services Institute, Inc.

The thoughts, ideas, trading strategies and anecdotes contained within this book are solely the work of the authors and are not meant to reflect the point of view of the Chicago Mercantile Exchange or any other futures exchange. While attempting to dispense the best possible trading advice, the authors cannot be held responsible for the use of the ideas contained within these pages.

Executive Editor: Kathleen A. Welton
Copy Editor: Pat Stahl
Interior Design: Edwin Harris
Cover Design: Edwin Harris

Published by Longman Financial Services Publishing
a division of Longman Financial Services Institute, Inc.

Printed in the United States of America.

88 89 90 10 9 8 7 6 5 4 3 2

Library of Congress Cataloging-in-Publication Data

Angell, George.
  West of Wall Street.

  Includes index.
  1. Stock index futures. I. Haigh, Barry. II. Title.
HG6043.A55 1987   332.63'222   87-3003
ISBN 0-88462-623-7

In Loving Memory
of
Clarence and Dorothy Ewald

Previous Books by
George Angell

Sure-Thing Options Trading
How To Triple Your Money Every Year With Stock Index Futures
Agricultural Options
Real Time-Proven Commodity Spreads
Winning in the Futures Market

CONTENTS _____

ACKNOWLEDGMENTS _____

We are grateful to Carlen Quinn and Jenny Gantner, our two ever-helpful assistants, for helping to run the day-to-day affairs of Haigh & Company as we spent hours trying to concentrate on the difficult task of outlining and fleshing out the chapters of this book. We also would like to thank our agent, Evan Marshall, for his faith in us and in this quite different approach to an investment book. We also are thankful to Kathy Welton, our editor, whose enthusiasm for a first-person account of the trading pits reinforced our own commitment to this project.

GEORGE ANGELL
BARRY HAIGH

FOREWORD

In the past five years, stock index futures trading has undergone a transformation from a promising idea that few on Wall Street thought would succeed to an enormously successful concept that has revolutionized securities trading in this country.

At the Chicago Mercantile Exchange, where the most successful stock index futures contract is traded, the volatile S&P 500 contract has captured the imagination of hedgers, speculators and arbitrageurs from around the world. In April 1982, when the contract was first introduced, exchange officials mounted a "Fifteen Minutes, Please" campaign to lure traders away from the more successful currencies and livestock pits. Today, the action is so wild you'd have a hard time keeping traders away from the S&P pit. With the Dow Jones industrial averages plunging as much as 86 points in a single session, the volatility and volume in the S&P 500 pit has grown at a staggering rate. More than 150,000 contracts were recently traded in a single day. What's more, the S&P pit will continue to be at the center of the action as the big institutional players, among them pension funds, mutual funds, risk arbitrageurs, banks and insurance firms, join in the fray.

For the public speculators looking for a sizable return from a modest investment, the potential rewards—and the risks—have never been greater than in today's index market. The amount of money changing hands in the volatile S&P futures market is incredible. Fortunes are often won—and lost—overnight. The recent surge in membership seat prices—they doubled in less than a year—reflects the burgeoning popularity of stock index futures trading at the Merc. Along with the popularity of the S&P contract, however, has come a change in the rules of the game.

A trader today has to be more aware of the pitfalls of this high-risk game than ever before. With this in mind, we decided to write a book about how the game is really played. *West of Wall Street* will give novice and seasoned traders a behind-the-scenes look at highly leveraged futures trading from the vantage point of the pit. Why are orders filled as they are? Who are the key players? What does it mean to double or triple up? How do you know when it's time to throw in the towel on a trade? In short, what are the rules the professionals live and die by?

Little has been written by the real insiders and professionals who buy and sell millions of dollars worth of stocks, bonds, options and futures on a daily basis. The writings about Wall Street have been left to the journalists, market analysts, brokers and gurus who make their living *off* the market rather than *in* it. There are many good reasons for this, one being that successful market strategies pay so much more than successful journalistic ventures. But without the insider's perspective one never really knows how the market works, or what strategies pay most handsomely.

We've tried to shed a little light on how money is actually made in S&P stock index futures trading rather than how it might be made on a theoretical basis. This is especially important in today's financial world, where the difference between a profit and a loss can often be measured, one way or another, in a second.

While only a few will ever experience real-life pit trading on a futures exchange, the lessons to be learned there are transferable to speculating in general. After all, if you don't understand what goes on in the trading pit, where every order must go to be filled, how are you going to understand how to trade? So it is our goal to bring you a vivid and easy-to-understand account of what goes on amid the yelling and screaming, bluffing and grandstanding. In the pages that follow you will find examples, anecdotes and rules that will show you how to trade successfully. This information is vital if you have ever entertained the thought of trading a single stock index contract.

Above all, we'd like to dispel some misconceptions about trading. For one, successful stock index futures trading is not a science, but an art. The secret does not lie in crunching numbers or purchasing software. The computer doesn't exist that can ferret out the nuances of trading. Much of what makes a successful trader has to do with judgment and experience. Intuition cannot be ignored. You must always be alert to sabotage from within—your own psychological temperament that might have you holding onto losers and cutting short winners—a sort of fifth column that often leads potentially successful traders and even seasoned professionals down the wrong road. In the rough-and-tumble world of stock index futures trading, you can never be certain that any one strategy is the one to follow. You must place your confidence in proven techniques that will ultimately make you a winner.

If we could sum up the gist of the book, it would be about values and attitudes—specifically, the winning values and winning attitudes that it takes to triumph in this highly competitive game. Perhaps more than anything else, *who you are* will determine your success in the market. You will be the one forced to "pull the trigger" on a trade. Your temperament will determine whether you fall victim to your own fear and greed. You'll have to decide whether this high-risk occupation is for you.

Five percent of the participants in the market earn 90 percent of the money; the other 95 percent fight like mad over the remaining ten percent of the profits. Indeed, most don't earn anything. So it shouldn't come as a surprise that in futures trading, above all else, the cream rises. The best traders—the brightest, the quickest, the most courageous— earn the lion's share of the profits. On the other side of the coin—the misinformed, the foolish, the cowards and dreamers—tend to go down to defeat. After all, futures trading is a consummate game of skill—not luck. And who among us who values rationality would want it any other way? With the smartest brains on Wall Street trying to win, who would doubt that the stock index futures trading is really a vehicle for the best and the brightest?

Given our volatile financial times, the likelihood of the S&P futures contract becoming the biggest and most successful contract ever introduced is quite high. So, far from being on the fringe of the investment world, S&P 500 futures are at the very heart. Not long ago, a *Business Week* cover story on stock index trading characterized pit traders at the Chicago Mercantile Exchange as "feisty daredevils who scream their lungs out on the floor of the exchange." You'd be surprised at how difficult it is to be one of those daredevils on a daily basis. This is their story.

George Angell
Barry Haigh

HOW TO READ THIS BOOK _____

If you were to stand in the visitors' gallery overlooking the chaotic S&P 500 futures pit at the Chicago Mercantile Exchange, you'd probably be confused, perhaps overwhelmed, by the spectacle before your eyes. Arms flailing, voices raised, the mob of 400 or more traders just a hundred or so feet away from the gallery might seem to be engaging in a mystical rite. The words and gestures might seem unintelligible, but to the professional pit traders there is a precise and understandable dialogue taking place—one in which millions of dollars can ride on the nod of a head, a single outstretched palm.

To make this financial shorthand intelligible to the reader who may be unfamiliar with futures pit trading, we'd like to cover a few basic points on the nomenclature of the futures market.

The traders who "bid" (buy) or "offer" (sell) futures contracts do so under a so-called "open outcry" auction system. This means that, in effect, every trader is his own auctioneer. He yells out his bids and offers to make his intentions known. Moreover, these bids and offers are yelled out in a very precise manner. For example, buyers must always state the price and then the number of contracts for which they are bidding. Thus, "Seventy bid on 100!" or "Seventy on 100!" means the trader is willing to buy 100 standardized S&P 500 contracts at a price of 70, the 70 being the most significant price since the other pit traders will know if the contract is trading at, say, the 245 level or the 244 level, or whatever. Accordingly, if the last price is 246.65, the entire pit will understand the "seventy" to signify a price of 246.70, or a tick higher since the S&P 500 contract trades in increments of .05, or 5/100ths—246.65, 246.70, 246.75 and so on.

The underlying value of the contract is 500 times the quoted price. Hence, at a price of 246.70, the contract is valued at 500 times as much, or $123,350. The value of a "tick," or .05 points, is $25. Thus, every time the market moves by one tick, all those holders of S&P futures contracts stand to gain or lose an equivalent of $25 per contract. The contracts are leveraged. This means that the trader who buys or sells an S&P stock index futures doesn't have to have the entire value of the underlying contract on deposit with his or her brokerage house. Hardly. The typical margin is about $10,000 per contract, or about four or five percent of the value of the underlying contract. As a result, even a modest change in the price of an underlying contract translates into a significant percentage gain or loss to the holder of the contract. This high leverage certainly adds to the excitement and opportunity for significant gain or loss in the market.

Returning to our illustration of pit trading, the sellers "offer," or sell, contracts by yelling out the number, or size, they are willing to sell followed by the word "at" and the price. Hence, "Eighty at 40!" denotes the trader's intentions to sell 80 contracts at a price of 40—again, the 40 pertains only to the last two digits of the transaction. Everyone in the pit understands the dollar price level.

The futures contract—sometimes called a "car"—is a

standardized unit which traders buy and sell much in the manner of a round-lot in the stock market. The term "car," by the way, originated in the commodity futures markets in the days when grain contracts were traded in units the size of railway cars. For some unknown reason, the term has persisted over the years even though the new stock index futures contract, which began trading in 1982, is nothing more than a legal fiction since it can hardly be delivered or retendered like a typical agricultural commodity.

Other common terms that may be confusing to novice traders are "long" and "short." One who is long is a buyer of futures contracts, whereas a seller is said to be short. One often hears a trader say, "I'm long the market" or "I'm short the market." The terminology means that the former has purchased contracts, whereas the latter has sold them short in anticipation of falling prices.

One other clarification for the novice reader: In referring to price, the term "double" means 55, the two fives representing the only price where the two numbers occur; "half" refers to 50; and a "quarter," understandably enough, refers to 25. The only other term which might be confusing is "even." That's the round numbers. Hence, if a trader bids "even," he is trying to buy at the round number—245.00, 246.00 or whatever.

For purposes of clarity, unfamiliar terms are defined when they first occur in the text. In the market, as in life itself, unfamiliar terms soon become second nature once you understand their meaning and incorporate them into your vocabulary. Due to the fast and furious pace of the futures market, these terms serve a useful purpose and are a part of the everyday language of trading.

Our intention is not to confuse the reader but to convey a sense of what really goes on down in the trading pit, where, after all, every order to buy or sell must be consummated. Whenever possible, therefore, we try to explain what was said and why—and, more importantly, its significance to the reader. The pit jargon, as complex as it may at first seem to a novice, is there to speed up the pace of trading. As reporters who have experienced the pressure of the pit firsthand, it is our intention to recreate the pit environment as accurately as possible. Hopefully, these explanations will lead to a greater understanding of how the market really works.

In telling this highly individualized story, the book begins on what should go down as a significant day in the history of Wall Street: September 11, 1986. For on that day, the market entered a new era. Above all, this is a story of how and why the "cream" rises in the market. Here, then, is the story of one trader's journey which we hope you will find both enlightening and entertaining.

PART 1

Understanding the Futures Markets

CHAPTER ONE _____

Thursday, September 11, 1986

It wasn't a typical day in the S&P pit.

On September 4, just a week earlier, the Dow Jones industrial averages had reached an all-time high of 1920. The pit had been bearish for some time and, as a result, there was a lot of confusion. The locals had been selling rallies for weeks, yet the market kept moving higher. A lot of blood had been shed on the floor during the last week. The locals were getting killed.

Perhaps today would be the day of reckoning.

We'd seen these breaks before in the bull market. Just three months ago, on June 9, the Dow slid 46 points. A month later, on July 7, it was down another 62 points. But what to make of this? The Standard & Poor's 500 contract, which was having a rip-roaring year, was already off 800 points on the morning of September 11 when some small locals started to bottom pick and rallied the market 50 or 60 points on five- and six-lot orders. The market was trading at about 235 when the rally began. When the rally ended it was up another 60 points. That's when I noticed something that I'd never seen before in the S&P pit.

Apparently, all at once, the hedgers had discovered the S&P market. A large, well-known brokerage firm that handled big hedge orders decided to sell S&P futures. Although the market had just touched 60 on a modest rally, the firm's broker yelled out: "Two thousand at a quarter!"

There was momentary panic in the pit. The brokers and locals looked at each other as if to say, "Did you hear that?"

The broker offered again: "Two thousand at even!" The response again was stunned silence.

The big players suddenly wanted to sell in a big way. But none of the locals or brokers in the pit wanted to jump in front of a cement truck, so they watched the spectacle unfold before their eyes. There we were, down 800 points already, one of the biggest down days in history, following on the heels of an all-time high in the stock market, and these brokers were selling thousands of contracts.

There were no buyers.

"What's bid?" the broker shouted into the crowd. He was trying to sell 2,000 cars, gesturing frantically with palms outward.

Watching this drama unfold, I realized that we were in for a sharp break, which would begin momentarily. Those big hedgers wouldn't be selling wholesale if they didn't have a clue about the market. The financial world just doesn't work that way. Sure enough, IBM, General Motors and other blue chips began to tumble. The averages started to slip. The market was about to get crushed.

"Two thousand at even!" the broker yelled. "Two thousand at half!"

Although many brokers and locals were trying to sell, this broker seemed to take the market lower almost single-handedly. Down near the lower even, some bargain hunter bid on a hundred cars, and the broker grabbed the trade.

That's what it was like the day the Dow broke 86 points. Pandemonium in the pit. I made about $60,000 that day. But, best of all, it was clear that tomorrow would be another down day.

Looking back, I realize that the signs were everywhere once we saw the open. Before the open, the mood in the pit was mildly bullish. On the previous three trading days, the markets had closed lower and bond prices—which most S&P traders watch closely—had fallen. So the feeling coming in on Thursday was that the market was overdue for a rally. Hadn't the Dow just closed at a record high of 1920? And hadn't the high been followed by day after day of declines? So the psychology in the pit on the morning of September 11 was to buy a lower opening and wait for a pop.

The psychology reversed 180 degrees when a tidal wave of sell orders hit the pit on the opening. There were no bids, so the brokers kept lowering their offers. As a rule, these lower openings provide an opportunity to buyers because they typically signal the end of the reaction. I nibbled a little and bought about 15 contracts near the low end of the opening range. We immediately rallied 60 to 100 points, so I sold out my position and made a few thousand dollars.

After I got out of the first trade, I just watched the market for a while. I started to worry because it was slipping again. I was particularly interested in seeing whether we'd take out the low of the opening range—the point where I'd originally bought my 15 cars. I knew from experience that if that low was taken out, the market was in deep trouble. That doesn't happen if the market is poised for a rally. Yet it happened so quickly that I knew the market would trade lower. In fact, upon taking out the low, it broke another 300 points before we could catch our breath. We were down 700 points on the day.

I remember commenting on this price action to my assistant. "Something is wrong here," I said. "This stuff is going to get tomahawked." That was right before the large wire house broker began shouting his orders to sell.

What really surprised me that day was the way in which the order fillers and commercials were giving up the *edge*— the difference between the bid and the asked price—on every trade. The market could have last traded at 75, but the commercials would be selling the 60s. They didn't care. When the big players are looking for fills, not prices, you have to watch out. What do they care about a tick or two?

When you see the commercials and big players selling with impunity, powering the market lower, as they did that morning, you don't want to be on the other side. That's an important rule to remember: Never fade. Never trade against heavy one-sided, commercial participation in the market.

I followed this rule when I saw the price action on Thursday. I knew that we weren't going to rally them, so I sold about 50 contracts and rode them down about 250 points. Then I more or less quit trading for the day. By the close, we were down more than 1,500 points from the previous day's high. We were looking at a record close on the Dow. I knew that tomorrow would be another big day for me. My best days are always the ones *following* a big break or rally. Even though I made more than $60,000 on Thursday, I knew that I'd clean up tomorrow if conditions were right. I wasn't disappointed.

A $100,000 DAY

I knew we had another big day coming, so on Thursday evening I went home determined not to let any outside influence affect my thinking. I refused to watch television because the news would be filled with remarks from analysts who didn't know what they were talking about. I also vowed to skip *The Wall Street Journal* on Friday's train ride. I wanted to reflect on what my experiences had taught me. We had had a historic plunge, there had been panic in the pit and I'd been drained emotionally and physically. So I set up a scenario that, given the right circumstances, would make me a great deal of money on Friday. I was hoping that the bonds would open higher before the S&Ps began trading. Given the strength of the bonds and the sharp 1,500-point selloff in two days, I was hoping for a short-lived, short-covering rally to start off the next day. This would drive out the weak short-sellers. Based on experience, I knew the market couldn't sustain more than a 50- or 100-point rally the next day, so I was prepared to become an aggressive short-seller on any higher open. (Actually, the December S&P contract rallied just 30 points to 235.80 off the 235.50 open on Friday, September 12, 1986.)

Here's what happened. The next morning the bonds opened a full point higher. Within 15 minutes they slid about a point. By 8:30, when the S&P market opened, the bonds had rallied back up by about 20 or 30 ticks. At that point, the locals who had gone home short began bidding their brains out and the market rallied. I tried to sell everything I could get my hands on. I sold about 70 contracts on the initial rally and would have sold a couple hundred more if it had gone higher. But it didn't. The bonds broke suddenly and the S&Ps immediately went into a fast market on the downside. If I'd kept my mouth shut, I could have made a half million dollars that day. But seeing my $100,000 profit emerge in less than 45 minutes, I started buying them back about 300 points lower. I knew I could get better fills, but I didn't care at that point. I just wanted the money. It's tough to walk away from $100,000.

TWO GOOD LESSONS

Those two days taught me a couple of things:

First, you can never say with certainty what will happen in the market. Witness the buyers who tried to pick a bottom on September 11, 1986. A number of traders kept averaging that day, buying more and more, until they averaged themselves out of existence. At some point in any trade, you have to call it quits. You can't say, "This won't happen," because it can happen, and it did. We lost close to 3,000 points in the S&Ps during that fateful week in September.

Second, you have to keep your eyes on the hedgers.
When you see the hedgers trading without regard to where
they are filled, you have to be careful. On normal days, the
commercials and arbs won't budge from their bids and
offers. If they offer 200 contracts at 70, they are not likely
to sell them at 55. When they lower their offers, you know
they are serious about selling. It means trouble is brewing.
That's precisely what happened in September 1986.

LOOK FOR SIZE AND VOLATILITY

I'd never seen such size in the S&P pit. There were offers
to sell 5,000 contracts on a single trade. The brokers trying
to fill these orders would send the market down 60 or 70
points immediately just by indicating the size. No one
wanted to touch the other side of such a trade. Finally,
when they realized they were moving the market, they
kept quiet and hit every bid. Whatever the pit was willing
to buy they would sell. A local would bid 60 on 100 cars,
and the brokers would immediately "hit" him, or take the
sell side of the trade. A broker would then offer 500 at a
half and another 500 at 40. You can imagine how the local
felt after buying at 60. The sell orders poured in all day
long.

How can you tell whether the big commercials and arbs
are moving the market? Just look at the volatility. Any day
with a move of 500 or 600 points usually represents a
serious commitment on the part of the commercials. You
also want to note the direction of the move. In the biggest
bull market in history, from August 1982 through August
1986, the biggest one-day advance in the S&P was 605
points. This seems modest compared to the Dow's advance
of more than 1,200 points over that period, and with the
S&P's single-day declines of more than 800 points on five
occasions over the past few months. Consider the implications if you decide to pick the bottom in such a market.

NEVER BUY THOSE SHARP BREAKS

Taking those lessons to heart, *never buy* the S&P market when it is down 600 or 700 points. Under those circumstances, the Dow could easily lose another 30 or 40 points in a matter of minutes. A 500,000-share block order to sell IBM, General Electric or one of the other blue chips would be enough to start the tailspin. With such selling under way, the specialists would have a hard time maintaining an orderly market. You could expect them to lower the bids by $2 or $3.

I'll never forget the pattern of trading that day. There's always a certain electricity on the trading floor, but on those two days in September, the air was highly charged. The nearby contract had been trading at a premium for months, but suddenly the December contract, with three-and-half-months left to expiration, was trading at a 400-point discount to spot. I saw this as a gift, and my instincts told me to go in there and buy it. So I did and—sure enough—it bounced and I made a profit. I got away with that trade because I was standing in the pit and could grab the profit quickly. I hate to think about what would have happened if I had not been standing there.

Later, when the market broke under the lows of the day, I remember thinking, "Wait a minute. That's not supposed to happen. Where are the big guys willing to buy these bargain prices?" They weren't there. They were selling. So the market became a very one-sided affair: *It was rising on one- and two-lot orders with 100- and even 1,000-lot orders hanging above the market to sell.* At that point, there was only one course of action: Sell.

The selling was something to watch that day. It just became more and more frenzied as even the most hardened buyers had to come in selling. Then it began to feed on itself. Finally, every buyer in the world decided to throw in the towel, and it became a bloodbath. The selling panic was palpable after awhile.

A CHANGE IN THE MARKET?

What happened on September 11, 1986, signaled a new era in the securities markets.

We traded about 150,000 contracts that day—twice the normal volume. But the *quality* of the participation also was different that day. It was the first time in my experience—and I'd been there since opening day in 1982—that we saw portfolio hedging across the board by a host of institutions, including banks, insurance companies, pension and mutual funds. In most cases, they didn't care where they were filled. They simply wanted to sell.

Now that institutional players understand the advantages in hedging, they are willing to use the S&P market to accomplish what they might have confined to the Big Board years ago. As a result, we are going to see more and more volatility in the futures, options and equities markets.

Consider the plight of an institutional manager who wants to sell stocks valued at $500 million on a day when the Dow is tumbling. Can you imagine the field day the specialists would have with these orders? They would lower the bids out of sight. So, in today's market, the institutional manager with a survival instinct will sell quantities of S&P futures in the Chicago market as a hedge against lower stock prices. When the market settles down, the manager will begin to sell off certain stocks in the portfolio. At the same time, he'll begin buying back, or covering, the short futures position.

The institutional manager trying to protect a portfolio from a catastrophic break in security prices tends to create volatility—a phenomenon that has been blamed for many of the small investor's woes. Remember that institutional selling in this fashion often sets in motion a chain of events that adds fuel to the fire. The big breaks set off selling programs. These, in turn, create more sell hedging and so on, until the move begins to feed on itself.

In my seven years of futures trading I thought that I'd seen much of what there was to see in the market. I've been through some crazy markets. So what do you think I felt when, all of a sudden, I saw something brand new occurring right before my eyes? The selling of 5,000-lot orders with no price in mind? Believe me, this was something new. If you've been around awhile, you know that the commercials just don't do that. That's why what happened in September of 1986 was so special. It marked a transition to a new era in stock index futures trading.

Looking back, I can see how instructive a significant market break can be. Fortunately, I was able to learn from the experience and adapt my style of trading. That's what made me a lot of money.

CHAPTER TWO _____

The Pit and the Players—
Understanding the Basics

If you are going to make money trading futures, you will have to understand what goes on in the pit—how the prices are made, who the players are, what strategies each group employs and the psychology of the floor.

THE MAJOR PLAYERS

There are four major groups of players in the trading pit at any one time: the commercials, the arbitrageurs (known as "arbs"), the commission houses and the locals. Each group behaves differently, tries to achieve something different or uses a different trading strategy in the pit. Each, of course, is a member of the exchange, usually the Index and Options Market (IOM) Division of the Chicago Mercantile Exchange. I'm speaking here of the Standard & Poor's 500 pit, although these four groups are present in every pit to some extent.

The Commercials: These are the large Wall Street firms that maintain cash ties with the New York Stock Exchange. Salomon Brothers, Merrill Lynch, E.F. Hutton, Geldermann,

Chicago Research & Trading (CRT) and Goldman Sachs are in this group. They do a big business with pension funds, trust departments, insurance companies and mutual funds. They have the institutional knowledge that most of us lack. Because they have enormous sums of money at their disposal and because they often have knowledge of "inside" market-moving information, the commercials can be the most formidable of the pit players.

The Arbitrageurs: The arbs are well-financed players who try to make very small profits on price changes between markets. If, for instance, they see the options overpriced at the Chicago Board Options Exchange (CBOE) in terms of the S&P futures at the Chicago Mercantile Exchange, they will sell options at the CBOE and buy futures at the Merc. Their trading activities are beneficial in that the arbs provide liquidity by creating markets. If you were to follow their actions closely, you'd find that they often sell into bull markets. Why? Because they are laying off their risk in another market. What they sell on one exchange, they immediately buy on another. If you want to understand arbitrage at its simplest level, take two markets that are exactly the same: If you could sell silver in New York for $6.20 and buy it in Chicago for $6.19—same contract, same delivery date—would you do it? Of course you would. That's arbitrage.

The Commission Houses: These are the brokerage houses that handle retail accounts. They are the firms that customers, who are not members of the exchange, must deal with: Merrill Lynch, E.F. Hutton, Heinhold, Lind-Waldock, the discounters and full-service wire houses alike. Their profits come from charging their retail clients commissions. There are, of course, firms that fall into each of the three categories—commercial, arbitrageur, commission house. Refco is one such firm.

The Locals: These are exchange members who trade exclusively for their own accounts. Most locals tend to stay in the same pit all the time. You won't often find an S&P

local going over to trade Deutschemark futures or options. There are obvious reasons for this: As chaotic as the trading pit may seem to those who see it from the visitors gallery for the first time, it is not confusing to the professionals on the floor. Except for those who come and go, the locals in the pit all tend to know one another and stand in the same spot every day. They are even known according to the trading size they can handle. The pit is very much like a microcosm of society with the haves and have nots, the rich and not-so-rich, the powerful and the weak.

HOW PRICES ARE ESTABLISHED

First and foremost, there is a buyer for every seller, and vice versa. As obvious as this may seem, you must remember that for a trade to be consummated, there must be a buyer and a seller. Customers often think that because they see a quote on a screen they can get an order filled at that price. Not necessarily.

First, the logistics involved may make this impossible. Remember, when you place an order, your account executive has to call the order in; the order then has to be conveyed to an *order filler*, a pit broker whose job it is to fill public orders. This may be accomplished either by a hand signal or by a *runner*, who runs the order into the pit. Only then, assuming you haven't entered a *limit* order restricting the broker to a specific price or better, can the order be filled.

Second, the last trading price you see on a video screen may become a bid or asked price once your order hits the pit. For instance, let's say you see the September S&P futures trading at 235.40 and decide to put in an order to buy one at 235.40 or better. The market may now be bid at 235.40 and asked at 235.45. In other words, the buyers want to buy at 40 and the sellers want to sell at 45. Will you be able to buy at 40? Probably not. Because there are 50 or 60 skilled pit traders who want to do the same thing, you'll have to settle for the 45 offer or not buy at all. Of course, there is always the possibility that both the bid and the asked price will be lowered in a moment or two and your order can be filled. But, barring such a move in the market, the locals and other pit traders are not going to let the public speculator buy at the bid or sell at the asked. That so-called "edge"—the difference between bid and asked—is the lifeblood of the floor, especially to the scalpers, who look for modest profits on every trade.

The size of the order will also have a bearing on price. You simply cannot trade big orders at every price level. It is one thing to find a seller willing to take the other side of an order to buy a single contract, but quite another to find a seller willing to take the other side of an order to buy 100 contracts—especially in a bull market. For one, relatively few traders in the pit have the capital to bear the risk on 100 contracts, no matter how certain the trade. For another, a large order, especially a large market order, is apt to either spook the pit—in which case the edge required by the floor will be greater—or to be broken up among several traders and be filled at different prices. Thus, an order to buy 100 contracts might be filled with 30 contracts at 40, another 30 at 45 and the final 40 purchased at a half. You must be cognizant of size.

Unfortunately, when you look at a price screen you cannot always tell the size of a trade. Was that a one-lot that just traded at 65 or two commercials going head-to-head on 500 cars? It makes a difference. The one- or two-lot order is going to be treated a lot differently in the pit than a size order by a big institutional trader. When the big money comes into the game, the last bid and asked prices are relatively meaningless. If the market is bid 40 and asked at 45, the commercial might offer 500 at 30 and another 200 at 25. In this instance, the big commercial *is* the market. But in reality, when they see this kind of selling, the panic-stricken locals who are caught long S&P futures will take the market down to even offer in seconds. They have to draw out buyers for their contracts before the commercials take the market lower. The commercials, simply by virtue of their size, can crush a price rally just by entering the market. Indeed, if they are eager to get an order off, they sometimes have no alternative.

All trades in the pit are established by open outcry. This means that every trader acts as his or her own auctioneer, either bidding or offering. The rule is that every bid or offer must be yelled out to give everyone in the pit an opportunity either to take the other side of the trade or to ignore it. Accordingly, the last bid in the immediate time frame is the price floor and the last offer is the price ceiling. Traders are not permitted to bid under the prevailing bid nor offer over the current prevailing offer, lest they be "off the market." But traders can bid higher or offer lower. Thus, if my bid is 25 and you then bid 30, you are the market; the next trader to come in with a higher bid, let's say 35, will then be the market. It works in reverse when traders are offering down the market.

If you understand how this process works, you can imagine what happens when panic hits the pit. If everyone turns bullish at once, the inevitable rally will begin. Those seeking to buy will have to bid up the market to draw out a seller. And if the bullishness is really strong, you will get what we call, in the jargon of the pit, an "airball." This means the market will be bid up in a hurry as the buyers all panic at once. Airballs occur when news events hit or when the pit psychology changes quickly and a number of locals—usually the poorly financed ones—get caught. At that point, they have little alternative but to either bid or offer the market out of sight. They must find a willing buyer or seller, depending upon whether they are long or short, or they will be unable to pay their losses on the trade. So, in answer to the question, isn't there always a buyer and a seller, the answer is yes. But to draw out that buyer or seller, the market may have to take a sudden rise or fall.

Were there buyers on September 11, 1986, the day the Dow broke 86 points? Of course. But many of them turned sellers once they realized the market was going lower. Moreover, once the large commercials came in with 5,000-lot orders to sell at half-point intervals, the buying evaporated. The result? The market crashed. Ask yourself this: Would you want to be a lone buyer in a sea of sellers? It is that one-sided panic that fuels the market. You'd have to be crazy to fade a move like that. Thus, when the market runs, one side will typically stand on its hands. The result will be an airball—if not worse.

THE ILLUSION OF THE TAPE

When the market runs, the speculator on the outside sees the prices move in a pretty steady progression—double (55), 60, 65, 70 and so on. But in a fast market situation, it is unlikely that actual trades occurred at those prices. More often than not, they were simply bids from buyers willing to pay that price. The way the pit operates, each bid must equal or exceed the previous bid in the immediate time frame; when selling, the offers must be equal to or less than the previous offer in the same time frame. Thus, if you bid double and I immediately bid 60, the market is at 60 because that's the higher bid. A second later, another trader might bid 65, another 70, and so on. The panic occurs when the pit becomes very one-sided. For instance, if the pit is overwhelmingly short and prices don't break, the sellers will have to cover their short positions by buying. In fact, the more underfinanced traders there are in the pit— and there are many—the more sudden the move will be. Why? Because they have to get out of the market no matter what. Sometimes that's what drives those fast moves.

I call this phenomenon, which occurs when the market runs fast and the prices are posted in an orderly fashion, "the illusion of the tape." Are trades actually consummated at these prices? With 400 to 500 people trading in the pit, perhaps a one-lot does change hands at every price. But I'd be surprised if it were true. The action in the pit is just too disorderly to have such a rational market. When pandemonium breaks out, don't count on the orderly progression of the tape to guarantee you a good fill on your order. It won't happen.

HOW YOUR ORDER IS FILLED

Every order to buy or sell a futures contract must be consummated in the pit. Customer orders are handled by brokers known as *order fillers* who normally work on commission or salary for the large retail commission houses. These orders are subject to the same rules and regulations as other orders. They are traded by open outcry, which entitles everyone in the pit to take the other side of the order. Public orders are often referred to as *paper* because they are written down on pieces of paper and sent back to the order desk. On the other hand, trading among members is *carded* on small cardboard trading cards. The trading cards are divided into two sides: blue for buying, red for selling. The public paper is divided into a buy and sell section.

When a trade is consummated between buyer and seller, both parties have to fill out their cards with all the terms of the trade. The buyer will fill in the seller's badge symbol, brokerage house, number of contracts purchased, trading month, commodity or futures and, of course, the trading price. The seller's card will correspond to the buyer's, with information on the opposing broker or trader.

A typical entry on a blue buy card might appear as follows:

8 SPZ 256.00 XYZ/815

Translated, this means that the trader purchased 8 December (Z) Standard & Poor's futures contracts at a price of 256.00 from a trader whose badge symbol is XYZ and who clears his trades through brokerage house 815.

OUTTRADES

When trading cards are handed in, they are keypunched and matched with those of the opposing broker. If the terms and prices do not match identically, the result is an *outtrade*, which will fail to clear. These trades must be resolved to the satisfaction of both parties before the next day's opening.

Every trade must reflect with whom the trade was made, the opposing trader, his or her badge symbol and clearinghouse number, the contract month, number of contracts and, of course, the trading price. The most important of these elements are buying and selling and price and size.

If, for instance, you thought you were selling June S&P futures but you really bought June S&P futures, you'd be in serious trouble if the market dropped 300 points. Not only would the market have moved against you, but chances are you would have bought back your short sale positions, which, in fact, never existed. So you would have another position to worry about.

Real problems are caused by differences of opinion on size. Was that five or 50 you sold a moment ago? There could be tens of thousands of dollars at stake in such an outtrade.

From a broker's standpoint, outtrades can be costly. A broker who fills 500 to 1,000 orders a day can make an excellent living on $2 a trade, but outtrades threaten that income. The loss on a single outtrade could exceed the earnings for a full day of trading.

The broker and local will often split the difference on a trade in question. At other times, when the outtrade is the result of an honest mistake, one party will make good on it. Since these misunderstandings can be expensive, everyone tries to avoid outtrades. In fact, many traders employ special outtrade clerks to catch errors and resolve these outtrade problems.

A trader can get away with sticking a bad outtrade on someone once, but locals who tried to make a living on outtrades would soon find that no one would trade with them anymore.

Everyone in the pit knows what the others are capable of doing. If you are a one-lot trader, don't expect anyone else to take you seriously when you suddenly want to trade 50 contracts. This is doubly true if you are new in the pit.

One day, a trader who rarely traded more than eight or nine contracts suddenly started selling tens, twenties and fifties, expecting the market to go down. It eventually did, but not in time to save him. The day he blew out, he was short more than 260 contracts. He cost his clearing firm a few hundred thousand dollars.

Apart from these aberrations, most locals on the floor are pretty careful about how they trade. Outtrades do occur, but considering how much information must be conveyed in a split second amid the frenzy of the pit, it is surprising that they don't occur more often.

When a public order results in an outtrade, the order is the responsibility of the broker, who in turn is responsible to the clearinghouse. Thus, every trade is guaranteed. If a public order is filled, the floor broker and opposing local must make good on that trade. How they resolve their differences is irrelevant to the public investor.

MARKET AND LIMIT ORDERS

When an order hits the pit, it is treated in one of several ways, depending on the kind of order it is. If it is a *market order*, which means it should be executed immediately at the best possible price, the broker will bid or offer it once or twice and then hit the bid or asked. The point is the order will be filled quickly. A good broker can get a market order completed in 10 or 20 seconds. So if your order to buy one December S&P futures hits the pit when the buyers are bidding half (50) and offering double (55), you should know that your order was filled at, say, 250.55 in about 20 seconds.

Why the higher offer and not the bid? Because the floor will want the edge on the trade and will only allow you to buy at the offer or sell at the bid.

A *limit order* will be treated differently. When you specify a limit on your price order, the order must be filled at that price or better—lower when buying or higher when selling. *Market-if-touched* (MIT) orders become market orders once the market trades at that price. As a result, a MIT order is subject to the same slippage as a market order. (For more on trading orders, see chapter five).

As a customer, you must realize that brokers are either working on salary or being paid just a dollar or two for filling an order. They won't spend a lot of time "working" an order, but will try instead to get the order filled as quickly as possible. That often means hitting the nearest bid or asked price. The attitude of the brokers on the floor is that they are just doing a job. Whether customers end up making money is of no interest to them. As a result, you can't expect floor brokers to go out of their way to help you.

Day Trading—One Proven Approach

Whether you should be a day trader depends on your personality and how much time you have available. To be a good day trader you have to understand the psychology of the market. You have to learn the significance of a higher or lower opening. You have to learn to ask questions: Why is the pit trading at a 200-point premium today? Why does it trade at a 100-point discount two weeks later? Asking questions can make you a good day trader.

Day trading is one of three basic approaches to the market: Position trading, in which a position may be held for months at a time; day trading, in which a position is initiated and closed out during the same trading session; and scalping, in which traders, primarily floor traders, try to make one to ten ticks on quick in-and-out positions.

Scalpers are sometimes known as *edge traders* because they always seek the edge—buying at the bid and selling at the offer. These traders undertake enormous risks in pursuit of small profits. For example, if a scalper makes two ticks on 20 trades a day, he will have a $1,000 profit at the end of the day. The risk occurs when the market suddenly moves against the scalper. I've seen the market free-fall 150 to 200 points in minutes—a classic airball. When this happens, the scalpers get killed. For the customer paying retail commissions, scalping is a sure way to the poorhouse. So do yourself a favor: Don't try to scalp a market if you're not on the trading floor.

Position trading is an altogether different approach. Position traders don't need to know what the players are doing. They look at prices months ahead. With the introduction of options on futures, position traders can even devise strategies that minimize risk, such as buying S&P futures and buying puts on those futures. With this strategy, risk is limited to the cost of the puts plus commissions. In fact, such a strategy would have worked quite well in the recent bull market. The drawback is that position trading ties up margin capital and involves a lot of emotional energy. Because the market is so volatile, a great deal of time is spent recapturing ground already won. What's won on Wednesday is often given back on Thursday. Besides, with low commissions, it's better to take the profit and then go the opposite way the following day. That's my strategy. You'd be surprised how the profits accumulate.

Actually, because I'm in the pit and not paying retail commissions, I'm both a day trader and a scalper. But for customers on the outside, I'd recommend not trading more than two or three round-turns a day. To be a day trader, you need a suitable market to trade. There are just two such markets right now: Treasury bonds and S&Ps. Both have the liquidity and volatility necessary to capture trading profits during the day. I believe in day trading, especially in the S&P, and especially if the market continues higher. *The higher the market goes, the greater the volatility becomes.* This means numerous opportunities not only to make money, but to reverse positions and recapture losses during the trading day. I cannot overemphasize the importance of this volatility. Volatile markets like the S&P and bond markets provide enough price change and movement during the day to make anybody a lot of money. But don't try day trading the slow-moving markets. If you do, you are asking for trouble.

The S&P market has never been more volatile. In September 1986 the S&P market traded over close to 1,200 points in just two days. That's $6,000 on a one-lot order. During the same period the Dow reached an all-time high above 2,100. What's more, the market will become even more volatile as it trades higher. Volatility is a function of price: The higher the price, the greater the volatility.

Imagine what would happen if the Dow went to 3,000. At that level, 30- and 40-point ranges in the Dow would be normal. But with the Dow at 800, such a range would be considerable. So volatility is just a function of price. When the Dow reaches 3,000, the S&P will have 1,000-point ranges everyday. There will be plenty of opportunity for day traders.

Actually, the market isn't getting any more volatile on a percentage basis. In terms of its standard deviation, the market is actually less volatile than ever. The standard volatility in the stock market is around 20 percent; it is currently around 15 percent. Imagine if the volatility were to increase. If you think the S&P market is exciting now, you haven't seen anything.

In the 1920s and 1930s stocks traded like commodities. It was nothing for U.S. Steel or Telephone to have a yearly range of 50 to 190. Futures and options products have diminished market volatility. Investors today don't have to be forced out of the market because they have a way to hedge their positions.

There is another reason why day trading makes sense. A daily tick chart of S&Ps or Treasury bonds will reveal a high correlation between today's price action and yesterday's close. This means that at some time during a trading day the price action will cross the previous day's close. Why take home a position if the market is going to touch the same price tomorrow? There's enough volatility during the day—300- to 400-point ranges, and sometimes more.

The S&P market doesn't have a daily price limit anymore, so a trader with open positions can be seriously hurt if a market-moving event occurs after the market closes. There is also the question of margin. Day traders rarely worry about margin because they are usually flat—without a position—at the end of the day.

I think it is important to be able to turn the market on or off. That's why I'm a day trader. When I go home at night, I don't want to worry about the market or tomorrow morning's interest rates. I learned to walk away from the market, turn off the switch and forget about it.

Your decision to become a day trader will depend on your personality, your psychological makeup and your willingness to dedicate yourself to learning how to trade. That's the subject we'll turn to next.

How I Trade My Own Account

You are better off waiting for the right opportunity. I don't expect you to trade the same way I do as a professional, but I think you should know what I look for and what I look at when I trade. The average retail customer cannot make money in the market by trading continuously.

WHAT DO I LOOK FOR?

Every morning, when I go into the exchange, I ask myself, "How am I going to trade today?" I adopt different perspectives depending upon the prevailing market conditions on a given day. Most floor traders tend toward a short-term approach. On the one hand are the scalpers and on the other the position traders. I'm somewhere between the two: I don't necessarily stay with a position during the day, nor do I thrive on one-tick trades.

KNOW THE TREND

"The trend is your friend" is my basic rule of trading. Are we in a bull or a bear market? The answer to this question will dictate how I trade. Although I might sell in a bull market, I will definitely limit the number of contracts I sell. The probabilities in a bull market favor rising prices, so why take unnecessary risks? I prefer to save my ammunition for the long side of the market.

I never lose sight of my goal—to make money. When I want to go on a ride, I ride with the market. In a bull market, prices will rise no matter what, so I don't try to fool myself into thinking I can sell with impunity under those conditions. Yet how many traders think that they can reverse the trend single-handedly with their sell orders? But the fact is, the market doesn't care if you are short two cars or 2,000.

DON'T TRY TO PICK A TOP OR A BOTTOM

A lot of customers feel that if they can't buy the low of the day, the market is not worth buying. Remember, *you are there to make money.* If you buy at ten and sell at 80, you've done well, even if you didn't buy the low of the day. After all, you didn't know what the low would be until after the fact. If you have the attitude that you *must* buy near the lows and sell near the highs, you are not trading for profit, you are trading for ego. You have a need to beat the market. I've been trading for more than six years, and until recently I never bought the low of the day or sold the high. It is much more important to look for trends: If I know which way the market is going, I can turn the situation to my advantage.

Countertrend traders who sell short in a bull market sometimes get caught in an upswing. The market might open steady or lower for days on end, renewing the short sellers' dream of lower prices. Suddenly a rally sets in, and they incur heavy losses trying to cover their positions. The hesitation in the market was just a way to weed out the weak longs. Even without knowing where the exact bottom would be, a trader could have made money by buying the market and riding the trend.

FOLLOW THE BONDS

I look for leading indicators when I trade. Treasury bonds, which open a half hour ahead of the S&Ps, often provide price leadership for the day. The stock market generally takes its cue from the bond market, so if bonds are up a full point, chances are the S&Ps will open higher.

MAKE TRADING DECISIONS EARLY

I won't initiate a day-trading position in the S&Ps after 1:30 or 2:00 P.M. central time. I like to look at the market in terms of probabilities and make my trading decisions early in the day. Then, if I'm wrong, I've got the rest of the day to get myself out of trouble.

I don't generally trade right at the open because I want to see some evidence before I put my money on the line. I try to put on my initial position during the first hour of trading. As time passes, I sometimes cut down on the number of contracts. This "winding down" is important because as time runs out, there is less chance for prices to move substantially. A significant portion of the day's overall price range is rarely created in the final minutes of trading. The time factor leaves little room for error when you overstay a market. In this sense, time is as vital as price.

Trade bigger size earlier in the day is my basic money management rule. If I take a position early in the day and I am wrong about the market, I can always reverse and try to win back any losses. Time and price are functions of the marketplace. If I am losing on one, the other will also work against me.

One day not long ago, I tried to sell for most of the morning. After trading near the highs for two-and-a-half hours, the market wasn't about to come down. Although I was wrong in the morning, I made money that day because I had time to reverse my position.

Another reason I concentrate on larger positions early in the day is that the moves are usually purer in the morning. In the afternoon, there may already have been a 300-point range, and the market can go anywhere. In the morning, however, the first real move of the day is just beginning. There may be only a 60-point range in the first few minutes, and the next big move will be a sign that the market probably wants to run in that direction. I wait for that sign before taking my position.

There are other advantages to making an early trading decision. First of all, concentrate on the first hour of trading. The chances of buying near the low or selling near the high are best at the open. It is also the best time to find trades left over from the previous session. Finally, by deciding early, I can position myself for the day's trend, so I won't be forced to chase the market.

I've advised against getting into the market late in the · afternoon because there isn't much time to win back your losses. Although it's true that the biggest move of the day often occurs during the last hour, it doesn't necessarily follow that one should initiate a trade that late in the day. I've described the frenzied buying that erupts when desperate short-sellers try to get out of their positions near the close. For those who are already long, this is an opportunity to cash in and get out of the game. But be forewarned: Anything can happen in that final hour.

This also explains why the Dow goes berserk in the final hour of trading everyday. The investors who sold stocks all day are now trying to cover their short positions. By waiting until the end of the day they have painted themselves into a corner. They have nowhere to go, so they bid at inflated levels, sparking tremendous late afternoon rallies.

Once the market has been open for a few minutes and the overnight orders have been filled, the day's true trend—or at least the morning's trend—will become more evident. It isn't enough to watch prices; you also have to watch the players, to see who's doing what, and the indicators, to gauge market sentiment.

REMAIN FLEXIBLE

The one trait that has helped me survive over the years has been my flexibility. I'm on my toes all day. I'm watching the players in the pit and I'm watching several price indicators—the Dow, the cash index, the tick, Treasury bonds and so on. I'm open to a wide range of signals and can adjust my positions in response to new information.

One advantage of my flexibility is that I never wed myself to a position. I'll dump my position immediately—even at a loss—if I see something going seriously wrong. As a trader who does size, I have no alternative. If I hesitate, I could compound my losses.

DON'T TRADE ON OPINIONS

Many people ask me how I deal with opinions, floor rumors and the like. Simple. I try to block them out. The best traders have a unique ability to eliminate 99 percent of the useless information about the market. I suspect that those with the most opinions are those with positions. Some traders who are long will find 9,000 reasons why the market can go up, yet can't point to a single reason why the market might trade lower. Can you think of a more pathetic way to trade? Talking a position is really just hoping, and once you start hoping you are correct, you probably don't have much chance of success. As a general rule, you can help yourself by avoiding all market commentary during trading hours.

I'm reminded of a day when a local who was known as a crazy trader came up to me and said, "I'm long 120 cars and I'm so confident the market is going higher that I'm going out for a cup of coffee."

I told him that it could prove to be expensive coffee. I heard floor traders talking their position before, and I'd always taken it as an omen. So, as soon as he left the pit, I sold everything I had at that point. Traders who tempt fate like this are asking for trouble. Moreover, in case of a break, I didn't want to be long S&P contracts if he had to get out of his 120 cars. Oddly enough, I didn't think he was wrong. After all, I had been long myself. But when people start talking their position, you know they are in trouble. It is the last defense.

After an hour of doing nothing, the market finally broke. Although I don't know where he finally sold his 120 cars, I know he didn't make any money on the trade.

SIZE UP THE MARKET

In sizing up the market, I think about yesterday's price action, how the market closed and the likelihood of more of the same today. Some of my best days in the market follow on the heels of big rallies or big breaks. September 12, 1986, is a good example. When the Dow breaks 20 or more points, it indicates that the market is weak. That trend will generally continue on the following day. By the same token, a big rally one day is rarely followed by a severe break the next.

In sizing up the market, I also look at whether the rallies and declines are legitimate. One way to tell is to see how fast they occur and how large the volume is. High volume accompanied by follow-through in the direction of prices can mean that a significant move is under way.

About once a month almost all the indicators will point one way or another, but things aren't usually that clear-cut. For instance, the commission houses and the locals might start bidding the market up. Then, when the whole pit is long, some commercial might offer to sell 500 contracts, unleashing several minutes of sheer pandemonium. When that happens, it's tough to find clues.

Generally, the market will tell you what it wants to do—if you know how to read the price action. One-sided markets want to get someplace in a hurry, but don't jump too quickly. The first rush may be nothing more than a bull trap that can lure you into buying the top. I've learned to wait for the drawdown before taking a position.

DOUBLING UP AND TAKING RISKS

If my first trade of the day turns a profit, I'm on my way to a good day. But if the first trade isn't profitable, I may have to double or even triple up. Taking additional contracts averages the cost of the two positions, giving me a lower overall buying cost or a higher selling price. The market will usually bounce or break at some point, so I can generally get back to breakeven with a minimum of damage. At that point, I exit the trade and start over again.

How does this work in practice? I recently bought ten contracts at a price of 85; then the market dropped to 70 and I immediately bought 10 more. Prices then turned even lower, so I decided to close out my position. On the next rally back up to 80, I sold all 20 contracts. I abandoned my original position because the price action wasn't encouraging.

I'll explain doubling up more fully in chapter sixteen, but for now let me caution that although doubling up works for me as a professional trader, my situation is different from that of the average retail customer. Because I'm not paying commissions, my cost is just $1.20 a round-turn. I also have the trading floor advantage. If I sense trouble, I can get out of my position almost immediately by hitting the closest bid at my size. I'm not afraid to double up in a bull market because there's a high probability that at some time during the day the market will rally. That will give me an opportunity to get out of my position with a profit. Even if the Dow is down seven points at the open, I'm not afraid to buy. The market is just weeding out the weak longs. People who are interested in short-term profits are cashing in. When that selling evaporates, there will be nothing left but buyers.

I might take some heat by doubling up, but I have a couple of things on my side: time and the trend. With five or more hours to go, the rallies in a bull market are likely to be a lot stronger than the breaks. When the rally comes, I'll take my profits and exit the market. If I stay in the market, I'll trade less and assume smaller risks as the day wears on.

Let's look at a typical scenario facing retail customers. With an hour left to trade, the stock market is surging upward. Retail customers are dying to get in, but should they? I don't think so. If the market has reached the top, how are they going to recover their losses by the close? What if the market's headed higher?

WAIT FOR THE RIGHT TRADE

Too many traders want to be in the market all the time. This is a mistake. The trader who doesn't lose money by taking reckless positions is way ahead of the one who has taken a position and lost money. Futures trading is a probability business. The probabilities suggest that it is better to wait for the right trade.

I'm convinced that if the locals and the public speculators had to go to a window everyday to collect their winnings or pay off their losses in cash, the volume in the market would be a fraction of what it is right now. Some of the big locals, for example, cannot bring themselves to cut down their trading. They feel they have to trade big everyday. It's like an acid transfer: A big local wins $100,000 on Thursday and loses it on Friday—or worse, wins it in the morning and loses it in the afternoon. The money is recycled day after day.

NEVER THINK ABOUT THE MONEY

If you remember one thing from this book, remember this: *Never think about the money.* The time to think about the money is after you are out of the trade. I know whether I'm ahead or behind on a given trade, but I'm not concentrating on the dollars involved. If I sell 50 cars, that's $1,250 a tick. The market might move against me right after I put on the position. I could lose up to $10,000 on a minor swing, but I don't agonize over it. I was prepared to risk that kind of money going into the trade. I'm not thinking about the money—I'm thinking about the trade. Should I sell more? Is the market going up on short-covering? Are the commercials serious buyers? Will the buying evaporate and the market break? I'm thinking about the trade. If it's a good trade, I'm going to make money. That's why I'm in there dodging bullets everyday—to make money.

The point is, you have to decide *in advance* what you can handle. Then learn to trade within your means. You don't have to trade the same number everyday. In fact, that doesn't make sense. It's all relative. If I have $20,000 in my account, I can trade ones and twos. If I have $500,000 in my account, I can trade hundreds. Sometimes, when I've had a good run, I'll pull the money out of the account and start over with $20,000—just to see how fast I can run it back up to $200,000. But I'm not thinking about the money. I'm thinking about the trade.

Many retail customers look for someone to blame when they get a bad fill on an order. Some call time and sales, demanding to talk to the floor broker or account executive. Others write to the president of the exchange. Instead of focusing on the money, these customers should try to understand the trade. They should pay attention to how the market trades and how it takes their orders. Once they learn to read the signals, they will become much better traders. Remember: Take care of the trade and the money will take care of itself.

PERFORMANCE IS EVERYTHING

Futures trading is a bottom-line business. The only thing that matters is buying low and selling high. No one cares *how* you do it—as long as you make money.

In many respects, professional floor traders are like professional athletes: We play for pay—high pay—and our performance dictates how much we'll make. For a basketball player like Dr. J, security is getting the ball in the hoop. For the professional futures trader, security is a good trade.

IS FUTURES TRADING FOR YOU?

A lot of people think of futures trading as a glamorous profession. They are lured by the idea of Porsches, Jaguars and overnight wealth. True, there is money to be made in the market, but there are easier ways to earn a living. The floor trader, like the professional athlete, is someone who sets the pace. If you are comfortable in that role, you'll do fine. If you are not, you probably would be better off doing something else.

How do you really know whether futures trading is for you? Open an account down to the floor, and start trading. Regardless of how you feel initially, give yourself a couple of months to grow accustomed to the ups and downs and to see how you cope with failure. If you are still around after two months and your share of losses, you are probably doing something right—even if you haven't made any money. Before you can make any serious money in the market, you have to learn that first rule of trading: Learn to survive.

CHAPTER FIVE _____

Trading Orders

One of the first things you will have to learn as a new trader is how—and why—to place buy and sell orders. In general, the floor is willing to take just about any order it can understand, but it will serve our purposes best here to discuss the most common types of orders and how to use each one.

BASIC TRADING ORDERS

Although there are variations on each, there are basically just two types of trading orders: the *market order* and the *limit order*. As the names suggest, one is done "at the market" whereas the other is done on a price limit basis. The market order, which is occasionally referred to in the pit as "going retail," is filled at the best prevailing price at the time the order hits the pit. Since there is always a bid and an offer, the typical market order is filled at the bid price if the order is a sale and at the offer if the order is a buy. In filling the order at the bid or the offer the broker is, in the parlance of the pit, "giving up the edge," or the difference between the bid and the asked price. This edge, usually one tick in the S&P, or the equivalent of $25 on a single contract, constitutes the profit that scalpers extract as the price of doing business for retail customers when they place market orders. That's why scalpers are sometimes called edge traders.

A market order isn't always filled by giving up the edge, but the customer is usually the one who relents when an order is filled. The sellers offer, or ask, and the buyers bid on contracts. For a trade to be consummated, one of them, either the buyer or the seller, must relent and agree on a single price, either the bid or the asked. When a market order reaches the pit, the broker may present it once or twice as a matter of formality before hitting either the bid or the asked price. Most brokers make just a dollar or two per contract, so they aren't likely to spend a great deal of time on a single order. And because their brokerage houses may hold them financially responsible for any outtrades, they try to execute the trades quickly, yet carefully.

A limit order to sell must be filled on a higher "or better" basis. A limit on an order to buy must be filled at the limit price or lower. Hence, if you tell your broker to buy one September S&P 500 futures contract at 231.60 on a limit order, if it is filled, the price will be 231.60 or lower. That is, it may be filled at 231.55, but not at 231.65.

Because the limit order requires the broker to obtain a specific price, the order is often not as easily filled as a market order. For example, if you want to buy at 60 in a market that is bid 60 but offered at 65, you may not be filled because there are so many floor traders competing with you for the 60 buys. They will be willing to sell it to you at 65, but because your order is a limit order, you have tied your broker's hands. Your order will be filled at 60 or lower—or not at all. For this reason, you can rarely, if ever, sell the high tick or buy the low tick of the day. Unwilling to give up that edge, chances are you will not be filled.

Now let's consider some variations on these generic market and limit orders. The most common types of orders are as follows:

- *market-if-touched (MIT) order:* This order becomes a market order once the specified price is reached. Thus, if you put in an order to sell one September S&P 232.80 MIT, the order can come back filled at whatever market price is established once the order is triggered. It may be higher or lower than the specified 232.80 price.

- *market-on-close (MOC) order:* This order can be executed only in the final moment before the close. As a rule, since there are so many day traders in the S&P market, there is a lot of liquidity on the close. MOC orders can be good or bad, depending on the movement of the market on any given day. For example, if you want to sell MOC, you are likely to get a good fill if the market has risen during the day and is trading near its highs. This is because there will be many buyers and few sellers.

- *one-cancels-the-other (OCO) order:* This order is given when you enter two orders but want only one to be executed. For example, if you want to place a stop order to sell, you may also want to place an order to sell MOC if the original stop is not hit. In this case, you would place both orders with the provision that one cancels the other.

- *fill-or-kill order:* This order must be executed immediately at the price given or it is cancelled.

GOOD AND BAD ORDERS

Order placement is critical. When initiating a position, you have the luxury of letting the market come to your price as opposed to chasing the market. So, when initiating an order, you may wish to opt for a limit or MIT order. In exiting the market, however, you may wish to get out of the position at virtually any cost by using a market order. It sometimes doesn't pay to insist on the last tick when you are exiting the market because the order might not be hit. For instance, if you are long and the market breaks, you might try to place a limit order so that you can get out on a rally. But if the order isn't executed you may have to sell at a much less advantageous price. For this reason, you are often better off "going retail" and just selling it at the market.

When you are selling, a limit order can place you at a disadvantage if the market touches the price and doesn't rise any higher. It sometimes takes a few minutes to get a fill report back, and by then it might be too late to act on the information. If the market breaks in the meantime you may wish to take profits, but you won't know if the order has been filled yet. With a market order, on the other hand, you'll probably know the fill in less than a minute.

As a local in the S&P pit, I sometimes see public orders that don't make sense. Let's say the high of the day is 40. Typically, the pit will receive a lot of orders to buy on a stop at a price of 45. Knowing the high is at 40, the floor traders will try to take the market to 45. Once the stops are hit, the buy orders will feed on themselves until the rally peters out. The same is true of any weekly or monthly high or low.

Remember, all floor traders follow charts, so they know that there will be stops to buy just above the previous highs on the charts and stops to sell just below the previous lows. On an intraday basis, this principle works the same way. Brokers across the country will be telling their clients to place stops just above the highs and below the lows. The locals know that a self-fulfilling rally will occur, so they buy everything in sight just below that area. Once the rally occurs, they will sell out their positions to the panic-stricken buyers.

Let's look at how this might work in practice. Let's say the market is trading up toward a five-week high. The conventional wisdom among members of the brokerage community is to place a stop to buy at the market just above the high. So when the public sells, the brokerage community, attempting to be responsible by limiting losses, will suggest a stop order above the highs. Now multiply that advice a thousand times. What you have is a ton of stops *all at the same place in the market.* The point is, you don't have to be a genius to know where the stops are. Simply look at a chart.

One way or another, the floor knows where the major stops are. They can see the head-and-shoulders formations on the charts. They can see the pennants and double bottoms and double tops. They know where the breakouts will occur, and they look for them. That's where the customer orders are, and where there are orders, there's money to be made.

What will happen if the market trades under a resistance level for eight days and suddenly breaks through that resistance? The market will run higher. For the floor, it is simply a matter of getting the market up to a level where the stops will be triggered.

NEW HIGHS, NEW LOWS AND FAST MARKETS

Consider this scenario: The market has traded up to, but not through a significant high for three or four weeks in a row and shows signs of another shot at the top. The locals will begin buying all the offers as the market approaches the previous high. Let's say the resistance is at 65. My strategy is to start buying in a big way down around a half. After that, I might bid on a single contract at 70. If there are any sellers at that price, my bid will trigger the stops and a buying panic will begin as soon as the brokers realize that they have 200 orders to buy at the market. They will start competing against one another to get the best price. The order fillers will be scrambling to fill the stops at whatever price they can get. In 30 seconds the price can climb to 70 bid, 75 bid, 80 bid, 90 bid, even bid—right up to the higher half. Of course, I'll be bidding with them also!

If they bid 90, I'll bid 95; if they bid even, I'll bid 10, and so on. They have to match my bid or go higher, and that's what drives the market. Of course, when the market doesn't need my help anymore, I'll become a seller and let the panicked buyers have all of my long positions. That's how I make my money.

Keep in mind that locals have tremendous power over the short run. Their buying and selling is well orchestrated and skillfully executed. If there are stops, they will try to get them. Days when the stops both above and below the day's range are set off can be very profitable for many floor traders who are on the other side of those orders. You can avoid this if you know when and where to place your stops.

CHAPTER SIX _____

_____

Changing the Rules

Did you ever wonder why Nelson Bunker Hunt went broke in silver? One of the big reasons was that the Commodity Exchange, Inc. (COMEX), the leading metals exchange in New York, and the government changed the rules in the middle of the game. The COMEX substantially increased the silver margin requirements and instituted a "liquidation only" rule, thus ensuring a preponderance of sellers and the subsequent market break. If rule changes can beat a big player like Bunker Hunt, think what they can do to the small investor.

A few years ago I used to trade T-bills at the Merc when the so-called "TED" spread—T-bills versus Eurodollars— was very popular among floor traders. The TED spread, which consisted of selling Eurodollars and buying T-bills, was considered a so-called "flight to quality." A number of traders, considering the banking crisis we were having at the time, thought that the spread would go out to 1,000 points, so they were enthusiastic about putting on large positions. But then the government stepped in by rescuing the Continental Bank and abruptly stopped the banking crisis. I suspected that the rules would change and traders would be beat out of a lot of money, and that's precisely what happened.

When the market heats up, the exchanges usually raise margin requirements. This drives the smaller players out of the game, which in turn reduces volatility. Moreover, the margins are usually raised when the market goes higher, not lower. As a result, it is the public investor who is forced from the market, since the professionals are generally short and the public is generally long. The knowledgeable players are usually holding enormous positions while the public is exiting the market. Typically, the liquidation of the public positions sends prices crashing and the market tumbling. In the Hunt case, the exchanges also had a "liquidation only" rule, which meant you could get out of a position but not take additional positions. Again, the market decline was accelerated because most of the public traders were long. The wave of selling drove the market substantially lower.

The silver example is the most notorious one to date, but that doesn't mean it won't be repeated. You have to be prepared for unannounced changes in the market even if they are not precipitated by government or exchange authorities. You might wonder when bonds are going to be meaningful to security prices and when they are going to be useless, but it is hard to predict. You need to look for early signs of a change in the market. I can remember a time when if silver would rally, so would soybeans—like clockwork. This happened because grain traders watched silver prices. It didn't matter whether there was a logical reason for doing so, as long as it worked. That was several years ago. If you monitored the two prices today, you probably wouldn't find any pattern. So if you want to formulate a rule, it would be: *Look for changes in the way the markets behave.*

Another example that readily comes to mind is the gold market, although in this case it wasn't a question of exchange or government interference—the market simply changed. When gold traded at $800 an ounce back in 1980, many floor traders in Chicago made fortunes. Many also lost their fortunes when the market went dead for the next three years. They gave back every penny and more because they failed to recognize that the market had made a fundamental change. At one point we were trading in dollar ticks in gold; then we were suddenly trading in ten-cent ticks. The money and the volatility just weren't there anymore. The market had just died.

Can the same happen to the stock market? Who can say? The clue to look for is a change in the market that you haven't seen before. If you see some price behavior that doesn't make sense, maybe the rules are changing. For example, what if the S&P traded in only a 100-point range for a week? I don't think it will—on the contrary, it will probably become more volatile in the months ahead—but it could happen. And if it does, you should be prepared to change your method of trading.

Far-reaching changes are occurring in the economy and on Wall Street that could have a significant impact on the market. The 1986 tax bill is one and the emphasis on portfolio management theory is another. Some of the people running these portfolios are neophyte traders with enormous sums of money at their command. Their presence in the market could cause significant disruptions.

During the latter half of 1986, we saw some significant changes. The ranges, the volatility, the size of the orders in the pit all pointed toward a new kind of market with new rules. One guideline worth following in this case is to reduce the size of your positions.

ACQUIRING PERSPECTIVE

One lesson to be gained from a changing market is perspective—you'll begin to see things differently. For instance, sooner or later, every trader will be forced to acknowledge that he or she is wrong in a position and will have to get out. So the new perspective might be one of learning to accept losses. Successful traders will tell you that taking losses has been their salvation.

There's a saying in the pit that goes: "I bought the first break, I bought the second break and I was the third break." Ideally, through observation, one can acquire this much-needed perspective without paying a high price. The point is, in this era of stock index futures trading, you can no longer safely say, "This can't happen. We've never had an 800-point day in the S&P before." We *have* had such days, and we will in the future. In September 1986, we lost close to 3,000 points in five days. Granted, the odds are against such tremendous swings in any given week, but when it does happen, it pays to have the perspective that allows for such events.

How can you gain perspective? Ask yourself: *How is the market acting?* Is it behaving according to your expectations? Or are there signs that something "new" is occurring?

Let's consider an example. Let's say the Dow is up sharply, but the S&P is having trouble gaining ground. Perhaps the market is trying to tell you something. On the first downturn in the Dow, the S&P may very well fall out of bed. After all, there's a reason why the S&P can't go higher on an impressive rally in the Dow. It is knowing how to spot these clues, these intangibles, that will make you a better trader.

I found it very profitable to look for certain patterns in the recent bull market. If the bonds were down following the open, I used that as a clue to buy the S&Ps and make money. I knew that the S&Ps would open lower on the lower bond market and that a rally in the bonds would push the S&P market higher. That's perspective.

An even better sign is when the bonds are lower and the S&Ps are steady. In a bull market, you have to buy that pattern. That decline following the open is just a way for the smart money to eliminate the weak longs. The S&P

market didn't break on the lower bond market because there was plenty of buying coming in to meet the offers by the sellers. This pattern becomes even more recognizable in the pit because the customers are typically selling on those steady to lower openings and the locals and commercials are buying everything they can. The locals and commercials know that the market will use the first sign of strength in the bonds as an excuse to take the S&P market out of sight. This kind of perspective is important.

Part of the art of trading is knowing how to spot these clues in the market early on, before it's too late to capitalize on the move. This talent is part instinct, part knowledge, but you need both to succeed. If it were simply a function of knowledge, every Ph.D. who trades futures would be rich. Clearly, this isn't the case. Without a feel for the market, traders tend to ignore the impact of the intangibles such as panic and greed, yet it is precisely these intangibles that separate the winners from the losers.

How do you acquire these necessary instincts? You have to immerse yourself in the markets. You have to spend time learning the markets, how they trade, their idiosyncrasies and how to react in a timely fashion. You have to watch the markets and then try to figure out why they behave in a particular way. There is no easy way to do it. Many novice traders think it is enough simply to purchase a trading system. It isn't. If you want to be successful with a system, you need to learn how and why it works, its strengths and weaknesses, when to fade it. By making the system second-nature, you are in effect creating your own system—one tailor-made for your trading temperament. As a result, you will feel comfortable in trading the system and will probably make money. All this is part of acquiring perspective.

Perspective is vital in terms of money management. If you are a five-lot trader, that doesn't mean you are as comfortable *selling* five contracts as you are *buying* five. I happen to be a 20-lot trader, but that doesn't mean I'll trade 20 on every order. It depends on the time of day, the kind of market we're in and a lot of other factors. If it is Friday morning and the market is running up, I may bid on 20 cars; with an hour or so to run in the trading week, I may not want to risk more than five or six cars. It only makes sense. Why risk losing the morning's winnings on a purely random move? And in the final hour of trading, especially on Fridays when there is a lot of evening up, there are a lot of those moves.

The same kind of perspective is required when you have a string of winning days. You can't just start with one- or two-lot orders and pyramid your way to a fortune in the S&P market without some setbacks. Yet how many traders, lacking perspective, lacking so-called "street smarts," try to do just that? Plenty.

I know there are plenty of smart people out there trading stock index futures, but the bottom line is: How much money did you make? It doesn't matter how much you know. A lot of people will justify losing money as long as they gain some knowledge from the experience. I'd much rather be stupid and make money than be smart and lose money.

So often in the market you'll hear traders say, "They took it against me." They want to personalize the experience, not realizing that the market is so large that no one player or group of players has any bearing on it whatsoever. Statistically speaking, your participation in the market is absolutely meaningless. So don't take it personally. Just remember that it is you against yourself.

CHAPTER SEVEN ────────────────

"Fifteen Thousand Dollars, Please"

When the S&P contract started trading in April 1982, no one knew if the stock index futures idea would take off. The exchange mounted an all-out campaign to attract floor support for this new venture. They made buttons and posted signs saying "Fifteen minutes, please." The idea was to prompt the floor traders to go into the S&P pit and trade the new contract for a few minutes each day. This influx of new traders would demonstrate that the S&Ps had both liquidity and volume. Before long, the slogan on the floor became "Fifteen hundred dollars, please." My first S&P trade cost ten times that amount.

The president and the chairman of the exchange personally led the S&P campaign. They were down on the floor handing out buttons and asking all of us to support the new contract. Their big pitch was that there were two hours left for the S&Ps to trade after the currencies close at around one o'clock. This made it a natural for currency traders.

AN EXPENSIVE INTRODUCTION

Like many other traders, I decided to take a chance on the S&Ps. Within minutes I realized that I had a lot to learn about this new market. When I walked into the new pit one afternoon, I saw on the monitors that the Dow was rallying. Misinterpreting the rally as a sure sign that the S&P was about to follow, I bought ten contracts. A minute later, the S&P broke about 150 points. I doubled up and bought ten more. Again the market broke. Then, when it broke for the third time, pandemonium prevailed. I quickly joined in the tumult and sold my 20 cars. I hadn't been in the market more than ten minutes, but I had already lost money. It was an expensive introduction to S&P trading.

After the close, I added up my losses. Let's see, 150 points × 10 × $5 a point. I'd lost more than $15,000! I was just trying to help this new contract get started, and it had already handed me a major loss.

Although I got off to a rocky start, I decided to switch to the S&Ps because the currency market had slowed down. The banks were bidding and offering thousands of contracts at every tick, and they were killing the locals. The S&P market had plenty of volume at every tick, but I was a little concerned about its lack of volatility. Until the S&P contract was introduced, the stock market had been fairly stable. But when the bull market gathered momentum in August 1982, volatility in the S&P became incredible, unlike anything we'd ever seen. At the Chicago Mercantile Exchange, 1982 marked a new era. Some floor traders did very well, while others had their heads handed to them. Those who survived learned that you can bully some markets, but not the S&P. It is a multibillion dollar securities market, not some little-known agricultural commodity. And, in the raging bull market, the buyers would take all you had to sell, and then some.

A HOT MARKET

Looking back, I realize that I hit a hot market at the right time. The S&P has become the fastest-growing futures contract in history, and I sensed its potential right from the start. It had to catch on, for the simple reason that just about everyone has an opinion on the stock market. The S&P is a vehicle for capitalizing on those opinions. Although the Kansas City Board of Trade was already trading the Value Line contract, it didn't have a well-capitalized floor population to support the new contract. The S&Ps succeeded because the Merc was innovative in capturing both the institutional and speculative business.

Markets come and go, so traders will gravitate toward the hot markets. Because there are a finite number of commodity futures traders, the more contracts that are introduced, the fewer individuals there are to trade in each. When a market appears to have lost its volatility, the traders leave it and go where the action is hot. That's why the Treasury bills, live cattle and feeder cattle markets are in the doldrums right now.

A PROBABILITY BUSINESS

Another advantage of the S&P besides volume and liquidity is that the probabilities are on your side in this market. I know that if I follow certain rules and avoid reckless trading, the probabilities will favor me.

Let's say the Dow rallies 25 to 30 points on a given day. I can tell you with some certainty that a good, strong rally like that is almost always followed by more buying the next day. The reverse is also true: After a substantial break, the market rarely regains the loss on the following day. Knowing these probabilities, I have some of my best days following a substantial break or rally.

I get a lot of clues about the market by watching the players in the pit. One day 13 or 14 new traders came into the pit. They were conspicuous not only by their neatly pressed clothes and nice ties, but by the little red dots on their badges. This was the exchange's way of warning veterans in the pit to be extra careful in trading with them and, if necessary, to help them card their trades. I was already long about seven cars when I noticed that the new traders were all buying. This was not an encouraging sign. Then, as the market began to rally, I considered the odds: It was very unlikely that these new traders would make money on their first day, so I didn't want to be on the same side of the market with them. I sold my contracts immediately, and about 5 minutes later the market broke 200 points. I got short and made some money.

What kind of percentages can I, as a floor professional, generate for my personal account in a year? Out of about 240 trading days during the year, I lose money on anywhere from 15 to 20 days. This averages out to between six and eight percent of the time. I might be down $20,000 at one time during a day, but I might come back and finish out ahead by $5,000. But when I don't win, considering the doubling up, reversing and other techniques I use to come out ahead, I really lose money. Although I always play the probabilities, the law of averages occasionally works against me.

When I lose money, I sometimes can't get out of a big position. That's the drawback in doing size. Although the S&P is one of the most liquid of the futures market, hundreds of contracts don't change hands at every tick. Rather, we go from price level to price level with hardly anything changing hands in between. This means I'm sometimes stuck with a big position. Sometimes I end up selling the low of the day, but that's the business. The alternative is to hesitate, and that can be deadly. January 8, 1986, comes to mind. That was the day the S&Ps had a range of over 1,000 points. The commercials were offering 1,000 lots at 50-point intervals. I made over $100,000 that day because I was on the right side. But if you were long that day, you were gone. The next day, more than a few memberships were put up for sale.

CHAPTER EIGHT

The Significance of the Close

Like the open, the close is one of the most significant times of the day because it tells you something about the market's direction and indicates the best way to position yourself for upcoming moves.

The market rarely closes on the high or the low unless there is really good bullish or bearish sentiment. Only on the sharp-breaking days, when the Dow is off 30 or 40 points and the S&Ps drop 600 or 1,000 points, will the market close on its low. But because we have been in a bull market almost since the inception of S&P trading, there are many days when the S&P closes on its high. If we go into a sustained bear market, however, the reverse will also be true. So the bias is toward the long side of the market.

HOW TO TELL WHERE TRADERS ARE POSITIONED FOR TOMORROW

The close tells you where everyone stands, where everyone wants to be positioned for tomorrow. Consider the implications of a close on the high of the day in a skyrocketing market. You get a wholesale rush of short sellers bidding the market out of sight at the close on such days. No one wants to go home short when it could open the next day a couple of hundred points higher.

Typically, the people who are short will pay up MOC. Yet, the good pit traders know that when the market is clearly running against them in the final 30 minutes of trading they are better off getting out at a loss than waiting to get out MOC. There isn't enough happening in the world between 3:00 p.m. and 3:15 p.m. central time to suggest any other course of action. Much more probable than a market turnaround is the likelihood of panic-induced buying by short sellers.

If the pit perceives that the rally is real or that cash bonds are higher, chances are there won't be anything for sale in the final minutes. So why wait if you are a buyer? *Buyers need sellers, not other buyers.* At 3:15 p.m. central time all the MOC buys will come in and the odds are very good that we will hit new highs. By waiting you will only pay a higher price.

150 POINTS IN FIVE MINUTES

Anything can happen in the final minutes of trading. I've seen closes with rallies of 150 points in the last five minutes. Yet there is almost no possibility that the market will break 50 points in the last 15 minutes on an exceptionally strong day. The odds are that it will close higher. So instead of trying to save a tick here or there, get out before the MOCs hit the market.

The people who are caught are going to drive the market in the final moments. Determining who is in trouble will provide an excellent clue to the market's direction.

You only have to look at the time of the day when the really big moves occur to see the validity of this observation. On a day when you have a big move—the Dow is up

35 points or down 40 points—a third of the real damage occurs between the open and 1:30 p.m. central time. The other two-thirds occurs between 1:30 p.m. and the close. When the people who have been hanging in there all day realize they are dead, they go retail and blow out. By that time, there are only buyers! Here's what I might do in such a scenario: If I'm long, I won't do a thing that might push the market lower. I won't open my mouth because I don't want anyone to think that I might sell. I'll sell only if somebody else bids. That is, I won't offer it, but I will hit the bid. That's because I don't want the pit to know that I have anything for sale. If I offer it, the pit might guess that I'm bearish and make me pay five ticks to make one. So when the market is rallying and I want to lighten up, I'll quietly begin hitting small bids. I sell a few at a time. When I finally get to where I want to get out, I'll wait for someone bidding size so I can sell 50 or 60 cars at a time. The beauty of my quiet approach is that once I'm gone (with profits), it's the other side's problem.

EVENING UP

Except on the days when the market really runs, most closes aren't very significant. Typically, the pit is merely evening up for tomorrow. That means the buyers are selling out their positions and the sellers are now buying. With so many players and so many opinions in the game, it is difficult to judge the implications of the evening up process. The only thing that's clear is that few locals want to hold positions overnight. There could be a host of reasons the market moves on the close. Perhaps the locals got too long and found no buying during the last ten minutes. So getting rid of their positions drove the market lower. Or perhaps they simply didn't like the price action. But when the market is trading at an extreme, you have to use common sense. If the market is up, the MOCs are going to be buys. So the correct inference is to run as soon as you can rather than to buy on the close. Conversely, in a down market, you can count on the MOCs being sells. So do your selling early and beat the rush at the close. This simple advice can save you thousands of dollars over a period of time.

DON'T TRY TO CHANGE YOUR ORDERS AFTER 3:00 P.M. CENTRAL TIME

Here's a simple rule that can also save you money. Think about cancelling your MOC order early on days when pandemonium is likely to prevail at the close. Most wire houses won't allow you to change an order in the final 15 or 30 minutes because it will be too hectic for brokers to go through their decks looking for MOC orders two minutes before the close. For that matter, you can't expect a broker to change any order—from limit to market, or whatever—in the final moments of trading. It is too hectic in the pit at the close. Come down to the visitors gallery at the close some day and you'll see why the houses impose this rule. So no matter what your position, or how the market moves, your fill will reflect whatever is there at 3:15 p.m.

PART 2

Becoming a Trader

CHAPTER NINE _____

_____

Getting Started— My Story and My Advice

HOW I GOT STARTED

I first got interested in the commodities markets when I went to work right out of college in a family-owned bank in Lexington, Kentucky. It was a $100 million bank, yet none of the employees had a college degree until I was hired in the trust department. My salary was about $200 a week. With my wife finishing her degree, we had just enough to make ends meet. I had a degree in investment finance, but we never studied commodities. In fact, commodity futures trading was a sacrilege among B-school professors—akin to gambling, I suppose. They preferred to talk about stocks and bonds—things that killed you slowly.

I noticed that the head of the bank trust department studied commodities prices everyday. He told me he was studying them because he was thinking about taking a flier in the egg market. I asked him why he wanted to fool around with eggs when the stock market was so much more legitimate.

He told me that if the price of eggs went up one penny, I would make so much money. Then he explained how to sell short—by selling the eggs first and buying them back later at a profit. When he explained how leverage worked, I started to listen real closely. That's when I got hooked.

There are several ways to make money trading commodities. You can buy or sell in any order, or buy and sell at the same time, in different contract months, a strategy known as spreading. The more I listened, the more interested I became. I took his advice and followed the egg market. When I got tired of eggs, I followed silver. I had silver in my teeth, so I could relate to that market.

I soon realized that banking wasn't for me, so when my wife finished college we moved to Wisconsin and I got a job in a brokerage house. As a broker, I had an opportunity to get paid while I learned the business. At the time commodities was a nasty word so I sold AT&T stock to widows— another job I wasn't cut out for. The brokerage house received lists from the New York office detailing the stocks they wanted us to push. At one point they were recommending Holiday Inns. A couple of months later, this same brokerage house became the chief underwriter, selling thousands of shares of Holiday Inns stock. Conflicts of interest like this are not unusual in the brokerage business.

Because the stock market was dead, I was able to talk my supervisor into letting me open some commodities accounts, although they were viewed strictly as a sideline. It was something the major wire houses did in rural areas to accommodate the farmers. But there was some speculative business, too. I soon had clients in cotton, silver and pork bellies. In my two years as a broker, I made a lot of mistakes with someone else's money. After I learned a few things about the market, I started to make money pretty consistently. I also started to rebel because the house didn't treat its employees very well. I began taking days off and wearing aloha shirts into the office. My boss wanted to fire me, but he didn't want to lose the commissions I was generating for the company. I finally got tired of the organization and decided to leave.

THE MAKING OF A CYNIC

I worked next at a commodities house that specialized in agricultural commodities, especially hogs, cattle and bellies. The Chicago headquarters would issue a buy recommendation for cattle to all the branch offices. I soon learned that before making a recommendation, the house would buy a limit position (the maximum number of contracts one customer can hold) to give itself a chance to sell those contracts to its clients. I saw this scenario played out countless times: The recommendation would come over the wire, the market would rally on customer buying and the bottom would fall out. We would later learn that the big commercials were sellers that day, and that our firm was among the leading commercial sellers.

The firm also used to hold hedging seminars for local farmers. We would get about 50 of them together at a Holiday Inn and explain some elaborate hedging strategy on the blackboard. Within three weeks, they would be trading their hedge. Farmers with hogs to deliver in April might sell three contracts in October to hedge about 100,000 pounds of hogs. If the price of live hogs dropped a dollar in two days, the farmers might say, "The hell with April. I'll take the $900 profit now." Do the brokers object? Do they remind the farmers that they needed to hold the hedge until April? They wouldn't object because they knew prices would rally and they could sell them at a higher price the next day. The farmers became traders—in and out, in and out—while the brokers made money.

I was too young to become cynical, so I decided to find work that I really enjoyed. I was 26 or 27 years old. My wife and I had just had our first child, and we were dead broke. The situation came to a head one day when my wife Mary cashed a check at the supermarket. We were overdrawn by four cents, so the bank charged us fifteen dollars and returned the check. When the store manager posted the bounced check at the cash register for everyone to see, that was the last straw. I wasn't going to be an account executive anymore. I wasn't going to push stock on widows or sing the praises of commodities positions that the house was fading. It was time to go down to the floor, where the real money was made. What did I have to lose? I decided to go for it. I resolved to beg, borrow or steal the money I would need to get started.

RAISING CAPITAL

My first step was to investigate seat prices at the Chicago Mercantile Exchange, the Chicago Board of Trade and the New York Commodity Exchange. I couldn't afford any of them. So I finally settled upon the MidAmerica Commodity Exchange, an exchange that specialized in mini-contracts and was then located on the second floor across the street from the Chicago Board of Trade. I managed to raise my $15,000 stake for a membership on this exchange by selling some insurance policies that my grandfather had left me and borrowing the rest from my uncle. That was in the fall of 1979. When I purchased the seat the following summer, I'd already made about $10,000 by cautiously moving in and out of the market on a day-trading basis. I was making a couple hundred dollars a day in the gold and silver markets, which were hot then. After several months of day trading, I realized that either the Treasury bond market was about to stage a major rally or the economy was about to fall apart. Bond prices were in the mid-50s then, I made a classic fear play and bought all the bond contracts I could safely margin. Fortunately for me and the country, the bonds staged a tremendous rally and I made $100,000—my first real money.

After the bond market surged, I made up my mind to go to one of the bigger exchanges. The Chicago Board of Trade had one good contract—Treasury bonds—but the Chicago Mercantile Exchange had all the best available contracts, including currencies and Treasury bills, which were really hot then. I also liked the dynamics of its marketplace, so I decided to lease a seat at the Merc for $3,000 a month. I didn't want to tie up a lot of cash in purchasing the seat because I didn't know if I would make it at the Merc. I kept my MidAm seat just in case. But the markets were hot then, especially the currencies, and I made a lot of money.

A $60,000 GIFT

I'll never forget the day I made $60,000 in Swiss francs. It was pure luck, a once in a lifetime thing. Here's what happened.

When I got to the Swiss franc pit before the open that day, a trader named Jimmy called me over and showed me his chart book. He pointed to a downtrend line he had penciled in just above the December Swiss franc prices. There were six or seven points along the line, and the market was scheduled to open just below the line. As I recall, the trendline came in at around 48.50 and we had closed the day before at 48.20.

The opening continued the trend down about 30 points that day—near 48 even—but the banks began bidding it up immediately. I bid alongside the banks that morning buying ten at even, then 20 at ten, and another 20 at 20. Pretty soon, the market was trading at 48.35 and I was long 50 cars. Within two hours the market had stabilized near the high. Then a few higher bids hit the pit at 37 and 40.

Knowing that the resistance was just ten points higher, I kept my fingers crossed. At 47 and 48 I started getting excited. I knew there would be hundreds of stops at a half. Everyone was holding back to see who would make the first offer. I decided it might as well be me.

"Fifty-one for one!" I yelled, waving my arms to attract attention.

"Sold! Sold," a chorus of amazed sellers yelled out. What kind of an idiot is going to buy the high of the day?

But my strategy worked. As soon as I bought the 51s, one of the brokers for the major European banks took the pit by storm when he called everyone's attention and yelled out "I'm 49 even bid on 5,000 cars!"

All hell broke loose. The short sellers scrambled. Some big commercials sold him 3,000 cars, and he got the rest off between 49.00 and 49.10.

As the cash market rallied and the locals hesitated, I decided it was time to lighten up my 50-odd contracts from down below.

"What's the bid?" I yelled out.

"Oh-five," a local yelled back.

"I'll sell you 50," I said.

He took them.

That's how I made $60,000 in one day in the Swiss franc pit. It was a stroke of luck that put me in the right place at the right time.

HOW DO YOU GET GOOD?

A couple of months ago I got a call from the brother of a friend of mine. He wanted advice on trading, so I agreed to meet him in my office after the close. He was in his early twenties, well dressed and clean-cut, like many new traders on the floor. A friend of his at the Chicago Board of Trade got him interested in the commodities markets. Now he couldn't decide whether to go ahead with his plans for medical school or to take his chances as a full-time professional floor trader. We talked about getting started and survival. "How," he wanted to know, "do you get good?"

"By not being bad," I explained to him. "By the process of elimination. You have to survive a learning curve." If you can break even on the floor your first year, you have a good chance of surviving long term, but most new traders don't want to hear this.

"You mean I'm going to beat my brains out everyday for a year amid the yelling, shoving and fistfights, risking thousands of dollars, to break even?" he asked. That's right. Harvard Business School will charge you a lot more and teach you a lot less about making money in the markets. If you plan to make futures trading your career, the hands-on experience is invaluable.

In many ways, futures trading is like an Outward Bound course: They give you a canteen and a pocket knife and point you to the desert. If you get to the other side, you are an expert. On the other hand, futures trading can be a lot harder than an Outward Bound course. At least with Outward Bound, you have the emotional support of your traveling companions. On the floor, friendship ends at the opening bell. The other traders *want* you to fail. They will even *help* you fail. If you are short 50 cars, they will gladly bid up the market against you just to watch the fireworks when you have to cover them higher up. They *want* to see you in trouble because, like gasoline on a fire, a big trader can cause the market to run—at least momentarily. You don't want to get on the wrong side of certain locals because they can make your life miserable. However, the floor is characterized not so much by personal animosity as by a kind of "siege mentality"—locals against locals or, more likely, locals against commercials. My bottom-line feeling about the players in the pit is: They hate you if you win, and they despise you if you lose. It's a no-win situation. For a new local trying to grasp the fundamentals of the game, it is twice as tough.

But that's how you get good. Surviving a year in the S&P pit is equivalent to Marine boot camp. You'll find out what it means to be mentally tough and what it takes to survive in the rough-and-tumble world of futures trading.

HOW MUCH MONEY DO YOU NEED?

Although many traders get started in the business through relatives or friends, others, like me, are self-made. I couldn't afford $100,000 for a membership on the Chicago Mercantile Exchange when I came into the business. I raised $15,000 to purchase a membership at the MidAmerica Commodity Exchange and then leased a seat on the Chicago Mercantile Exchange International Monetary Market for $3,000 a month.

If you want to become a floor trader in the S&P market today, you'll need $70,000 to $80,000 just to get in the game. When you lease (the current rates are about $1,000 a month), the Merc requires you to post at least $50,000, which you cannot use for margin. The rest is your trading capital. If you want to purchase a seat, it will cost you about $130,000 for the Index and Options Market (IOM) membership. Trading capital will be extra, of course. I suppose you could start with less money, but the odds against making it on a thin bankroll are high. Trading is difficult enough without worrying about capital.

THE ADVANTAGES OF HAVING YOUR OWN MEMBERSHIP

Savings on commissions are a major advantage of buying or leasing a seat and becoming a full-time professional pit trader. I pay only $1.20 per round-turn to trade S&Ps. If you aren't in the pit executing the trade yourself, you'll have to pay a broker about $5 per round-turn to do it for you. But without the advantage of an exchange membership, many public customers even with discounters are paying $50 or more per round-turn. When you factor in these commission costs, futures trading is not a *zero sum game*, but a *negative sum game*. So if you are a full-time S&P trader—whether you live in New York or Los Angeles— you might consider buying or leasing a seat.

There is another advantage in having your own exchange membership. If you trade from the pit, you enjoy immediate liquidity. The pit traders, after all, make the prices by bidding (buying) and asking or offering (selling) by open outcry in the pit. The price quote on the screen in a brokerage house in Phoenix or Boston could be a minute or more behind the pit—and in futures trading that can be a lifetime. Even with rapid telecommunications, the market can be 100 points away from the disseminated price when an order hits the pit.

Another advantage the floor has is knowledge of the players. In the pit, you can actually see whether a large commercial like Salomon Brothers is bidding the market up on a 500-lot or whether undercapitalized locals are bidding it up one lot at a time. There's a difference. And once you understand the roles of the major players, you'll see why this information is so important. As a full-time professional, I won't trade from off the floor. I know many traders do, and quite a few of them are successful. It's just not my game.

The Psychological Component —Acquiring the Winning Attitude

If there's one thing I've learned from my years on the floor, it is the importance of a winning attitude. Straightforwardness can be deadly in some business environments, but the floor is a perfect democracy: Every trader is as good as his or her last trade. You learn to think on your feet.

IT DOESN'T TAKE BRAINS

Although there may be a few geniuses on the floor, most good traders aren't all that smart. I don't have an outstanding I.Q., so I know that it doesn't take extraordinary brains to make money. The secret of the game is recognizing the truth and acting on it. And you don't have to be a genius to do that.

People sometimes say to me, "Gee, you are awfully cocky." I am. So was Muhammed Ali. He had confidence in himself—that winning attitude. He also knew how to promote himself. What's more, he delivered on what he was saying. He beat every contender who ever climbed into the ring with him.

When Ali was in his prime, my dad would bet against him fight after fight. He lost thousands of dollars betting that Ali was due for a fall. He knew that he was going to lose, but he liked thinking that just once Ali would get his clock cleaned.

The same kind of envy exists in the futures business. You might think that I'm cocky, but you would be too if you were making half a million dollars a year. The best traders have that self-confidence. They need it just to survive. But they also have the ability to face up to reality. That's what separates the winners from the losers. If the market goes against you, you have to pull the plug.

DO YOU HAVE THE MONEY?

The people who make the most money trading futures are the ones who can afford to lose it. How often have you been forced out of a position because you found yourself overleveraged? Leverage is a two-edged sword: It can work for you or against you. Because of the leverage, when you enter a position you have to give yourself plenty of leeway; otherwise, you could be forced out of a good position.

WHAT ARE THE ODDS YOU ARE GOING TO MAKE MONEY?

Let's say you've been paper trading for six months and have never lost money. You decide to quit your job and begin a career as a full-time commodities speculator. After a month of trading, and some painful losses, you decide never to trade again.

Chances are, like many would-be speculators before you, you have a tendency to take your losses personally. You've become a victim of your own negative psychology. One of the big secrets in this business, whether you trade on or off the floor, is that *you can never take losses personally*. The most important determinant of success is how you handle failure. I'm a full-time, professional speculator, but you wouldn't believe how many times a day I fail. I must make a thousand decisions during the day: Do I buy now? Do I sell? Can I get filled where I want to get filled? Can I buy at 20 and sell at 40? Can I sell at 40 and buy at 20? If I'm wrong, can I bounce back? How do you put a losing trade out of your mind? Most people can't. Anybody can handle success. But you'll have to learn to deal with failure if you want to become a successful trader.

BEWARE OF PAPER TRADING

Let me tell you something: Paper trading isn't worth the paper it's done on, simply because there is no money involved. You are a lot different when your chips are on the table. With nothing at stake, you can sit back and look at a quote machine with equanimity. When there is no money involved, you can sit back with a pad and pencil and follow technical indicators. You can even take time away from the market and go to the kitchen for a sandwich. Try selling a hundred S&Ps and see if you are interested in eating.

Contrary to popular belief, there is no easy money to be made in the futures market. Public customers think we floor traders make all the money. That's a myth. For every person who makes a lot of money in the futures market, there are hundreds who are blown out every month. You never hear about them because they are back working for a living.

DON'T GET EMOTIONALLY TIED TO A PARTICULAR MARKET—OR TRADE

I know floor people who will never walk out of the feeder cattle pit. Others like the grain markets because they were raised on a farm. I'm different. I'm not in there for emotional or sentimental reasons. I'm in there to make money.

That means I'll go to whatever market I think is best. To me, it is strictly a numbers game.

How often have you purchased a contract at ten in the morning thinking you would sell it at one in the afternoon, and then, three weeks later, found you had seven contracts that you wouldn't think of selling because you are too deep in the hole? So, instead of doing the correct thing and taking the initial $500 loss, you find that you are out $4,000 and holding onto a loser. As a result, you become married to the position. Your attitude is suddenly one of intransigence. "I'm hanging on no matter what my broker says. I don't care if the kids can't go to camp this summer." This attitude stems from an emotional involvement between you and the market, although it is an entirely one-sided affair. The market doesn't care, after all.

THE STORY OF HAL

About a year ago, I started a phone service on the floor for providing information to a select group of traders. I would write out market comments from my vantage point in the pit and hand them to my assistant who would then give them to our telephone clerk. I thought this was an innovative way to give my customers an edge.

I had a client, Hal, who subscribed to the service. He was relatively new to the futures market and had been doing quite well. He called me one afternoon and reported that he'd had his best day ever in the market. He said that he planned to make a million dollars in the market and had a solid four-month track record to prove his point. He wasn't just talking. He was following my comments and doing fine.

One day Hal made a critical mistake. He decided, for whatever reason, to pull out all the stops and make a stand. It was as if he *had* to win that day no matter what. I, on the other hand, was having a moderately bad day. I'd gone short and the market went against me. A typical client of mine would have ended the day with a $600 or $700 loss—nothing serious. Hal was a different story. He broke every rule. He traded big numbers, he got whipsawed five or six times. The experience so destroyed him that he never came back into the market. He did it to himself, of course, and I think he realized that.

What happened to Hal illustrates what often happens to public customers. Hal was like a knight in shining armor who met his first fire-breathing dragon. And it sent him running.

Hal called me after it happened. It had been fun, he explained, but trading wasn't for him. He was clearly destroyed. What had happened? If it were simply a question of money, he would have stopped after the first or second loss that day. Instead, he started breaking all the rules. He lost his discipline and made the trades a personal vendetta.

Instead of doing ones and twos—his typical market size—Hal started doing fives and sixes. Then, after a few losses back and forth, he made an emotional commitment and put all his chips on the table. "It's me or the market," he seemed to say, and the market wins those contests every time.

People get emotional about money. The rules say you should have discipline, but when your money is on the line you are going to get emotional. I can relate to what happened to Hal, but I'm also prepared for the inevitable downside of trading—namely, that fate is going to deal me some bad days. You don't know it going in. To be successful, you have to realize that the probabilities are going to work against you at times.

Still, events tend to cancel one another out over time. Some days you load up and catch the entire move. On other days, like the day the Challenger blew up and I lost $100,000, it works the other way. These things happen. You live and go forward.

THE PSYCHOLOGICAL PITFALLS

Futures trading is the ultimate psychological game—a game of terror, some might say. The floor will do everything in its power to intimidate you, but it finally comes down to you against yourself. How you deal with failure will determine what kind of trader you'll be. Think about this before you decide to trade. Can you deal with adversity? Can you take the heat?

We all have bad days, but when you have one in the futures market, you can bet it will cost you a lot of money. The law of averages suggests that every trader who stays around long enough is going to get obliterated in the market at least once. You should think about how you will deal with that situation before it happens.

Successful traders know that they are going to have bad days when the law of averages catches up with them. They also know that *how they react to a serious loss will teach them the lessons that will make them money.* Unfortunately, for a lot of novice traders who can't accept a big loss, the experience will end their career. They will never again trade commodities, futures or options.

Some of the psychological traits that are at work in reaching such a decision are standard. If you see them in yourself, step back from the experience and try to sort things out.

HOW TO COPE WITH THE PSYCHOLOGICAL PRESSURE

In reading this, you may be thinking, "Yes, this has happened to me. I've gotten in over my head and made mistakes." Well, it happens to everyone—even professionals. The only difference is that the professionals deal with the pressure daily, whereas the inexperienced investor may be new at coping with market-oriented stress.

One way to maintain your equilibrium under pressure is to remember that you are only as good as your last trade. No matter how much money you've made, you start anew each day at square one. The market doesn't know that you might be the best trader in the world, and it doesn't really care. So try to cultivate a little humility. Having made money in soybeans, think twice before you decide to trade in sugar. Try also to stick to the fundamentals: If you have a loss and the market isn't going your way, get out. Then start over again.

MONEY MANAGEMENT PSYCHOLOGY

Nowhere is it more important to understand the trader's temperament than when it comes to money management. Most books on trading suggest limiting your losses to a certain percentage of your risk capital. What matters here is not the general guideline, but how your mind works once you've incurred a loss.

Consider the following situation: If you have $10,000 to risk and you lose $7,000, don't go to the bank to take out a loan. Risk only what you can safely afford to lose. Your mind works differently when you are under pressure. When you are worried about your losses, when you are feeling pressured at home or on the job, you shouldn't trade. You are going to think differently during those periods. Your parameters and your assumptions about the market are going to be different, and you are going to make mistakes.

It is best to trade when you are comfortable, when you are margined properly and when you are in a winning state of mind. An individual who has a car payment due in two weeks and a house payment due in three weeks is apt to look for a quick profit. That is not a winning attitude.

TRADING SYSTEM PSYCHOLOGY

Trading systems in themselves are neither good nor bad. The important thing is how they are used. Everyone needs some sort of system, no matter how informal or simple, in order to develop discipline. This is where the psychological factors enter into the picture. There are two main drawbacks to all systems. Both are important keys to your success.

First, no system, no matter how mechanical, can eliminate human emotion. Why, then, have a system? Because they are mechanical. They are designed to help you take the difficult trades—the painful ones that your judgment will tell you you shouldn't take. This leads us to the "pain principle," which states that the more difficult a trade is to take, the more likely it is to succeed. The easy trades are apt to turn into losers; the difficult trades are apt to develop into winners. This is a paradox of the market.

Assume that you've been trading for five years and have lost money. You decide to purchase a trading system and let the system call the shots. The problem is, you still *have to pick up the phone and call in the orders.* All the system does is allow you to blame someone else. When you lose money, the tendency is to stop using the system and start calling the shots by yourself again. You feel in control again. If you lose money this time, you have no one to blame but yourself.

The second point is that most people won't follow a system, no matter how good it is. If I gave you a system that would make you a millionaire in two years—provided that you stuck to it religiously—I'll bet that in six months you wouldn't be following it, and you probably wouldn't be making money. Why? A system is a total commitment— you have to follow it all the time. Very few people have that discipline.

What are you going to do when your system loses money three days in a row? Chances are, you will abandon it.

But six months from now, that very system might give you a $100,000 day. If you have been trading futures for any length of time, you have probably purchased systems and switched systems on several occasions. Few people can stay with a system for a year or more. Yet it's not the system that's at fault—it's the user, who doesn't have the perspective and discipline to stay with a system during the inevitable periods of adversity.

CHAPTER ELEVEN _____

The Trading System— Taking the Disciplined Approach

As I mentioned in the last chapter, you'll probably want to use some sort of system. As a professional, I follow a system that suits my purposes in the pit and my attitude toward the market. Unless you are going to be standing next to me in the S&P pit, you, the public investor, shouldn't try to play my game. The system you choose has to fit your circumstances and your individual temperament.

WHAT'S A SYSTEM?

A system is an approach to trading. There are systems based on moving averages, oscillators, relative strength and even sunspots. A system should reflect a self-adjusting bias and be flexible. The more rigid a system is, the more likely it is to get you in trouble. A system also should incorporate guidelines for trading. One of the tenets of day trading is never to carry a position overnight. Long-term systems reflect a different point of view.

DISCIPLINE AND A POINT OF VIEW

The value of a system is that it builds discipline. Despite what you sometimes hear, there are many good systems that will make you money. Most traders, however, won't follow a system. The first time they have a series of losses, they give up on it. The irony is that *systems are more likely to achieve sustained profits right after they sustain several losses.* Although it is best to trade such a system right after a drawdown, few people are willing to throw good money after bad.

A good system also gives you a point of view on the market. Nothing is more pathetic than a trader picking numbers out of the air: "I don't know why I bought it there. It looked like it wanted to go up." That's an attitude you don't want to cultivate. If you trade based on how the market "looks," you are going to lose. The market *always* looks the most bullish at the top and the most bearish at the bottom. We see players trading by the seats of their pants everyday. Most of the time, they are trading on sheer emotion. They usually are late in recognizing the move. So they are always buying tops and selling bottoms. Once the word is out, the information becomes meaningless. "If I'd known the market was about to break a hundred points, I wouldn't have bought it then. Instead, I ended up selling two ticks off the bottom."

You can't trade like that. You can't guess—not if you want to win. The key is knowing the signs, letting the market tell you where it wants to go, well before the move is under way. A good system helps you concentrate on vital signals and disregard useless information.

MY SYSTEM AND YOURS

As I've mentioned, my method of trading is geared toward my particular situation. Because I'm a member of the exchange, I don't pay commissions, just a modest transaction fee. I'm playing a different game than the typical retail customer. I can play the customer's game if I want to, but the customer who tries to play my game is at a severe disadvantage. Paying commissions, depending on brokers to place an order and waiting for an order to be filled all militate against the customer's success.

The hallmark of my system is its inherent flexibility. On days when the market shows signs of a sustained move, I might trade several hundred contracts; on days when the liquidity dries up, I might limit myself to ten contracts; during slow periods I stay out of the market entirely. I won't risk getting caught in a position without someone to take the other side.

Will my precise method of trading work for you? I don't think so. In fact, it will only give you bad habits if you try it from the outside. If you have a bad day and try to double up and reverse as I do, you'll regret it.

I don't perform brain surgery on weekends, so why should anyone who isn't a stock index professional try to play market maker during the week? You must have a perspective on what you're trying to do: You are trying to take money out of my pocket. In the market there is a loser for every winner—or, more likely, many small losers for a few big winners. Because every order flows through the pit, chances are that when you win you are taking money from the professionals, not other customers.

In designing a system, remember that you are going to have to beat me by playing a game that you can win.

Scalping, for example, is not a game customers are likely to win. Scalpers in the pit, most of them locals, trade in and out all day long for two- or three-tick profits. This is enormously difficult, especially when the market is running. A scalper can make money for six months in a row and lose it all during a single trading session. So leave the scalping to the professionals. On the other hand, you have to address the question of overnight trading in a market as volatile as the S&P. It doesn't make sense for me to hold positions overnight, but if your perspective on the market is different from mine, it might make sense to you. All in all, duration is a matter of perspective.

YOUR OWN TEMPERAMENT

A system may be good for one trader but bad for another. A system has to reflect the trader's attitude toward risk. People who can sit on paper losses may be able to use a system that requires them to take a lot of heat. Others have trouble sitting on profits. At the first sign of a profit, they have to get out of the market. This leads to small profits and large losses—contrary to the conventional wisdom of riding profits and cutting losses. The professionals know to cut losses instinctively, but public traders are sometimes slow to learn this simple, yet vital, lesson. Be sure to select a system that prompts you to use sound trading practices and fits your personality.

THE "PAIN PRINCIPLE"

The "pain principle" is a well-worn concept in the futures market. Essentially, the harder a trade is to take, the greater the likelihood it will be a winner. That's one reason I'm not reluctant to share my trading secrets. I really don't think enough people will follow them to influence the market against me. Most traders will continue to act emotionally when their money is on the line, and most will continue to make mistakes regardless of the quality of the information they have. I saw this when I had my phone service. Traders paid me hundreds of dollars a month for information they were unwilling to use. Why? Too much pain. They wanted the easy trades. A few, in fact, did the opposite of what I told them! For example, at one point in the bull market, I put out the following comment: "Do not sell this market under any circumstances!" Yet some of my clients sold. The market was going up day after day with no sign of a top. The commercials, locals and commission houses were buying.

Afterwards, when I asked a few clients why they had lost money, they admitted that they'd sold it. When I asked why, the inevitable comment was, "Oh, I don't know. I thought it had gone up far enough." Far enough for what? I wondered.

Meanwhile, from my vantage point in the pit, I could see what the big players were up to. Salomon Brothers, Refco, Merrill Lynch, Goldman Sachs, E.F. Hutton, C.R.T. and the rest were buying everything they could get their hands on. Would you want to fade that?

That's where a system can help. Forget the pain, just take the trade. Leave the second-guessing to someone else. That's how to overcome the pain principle.

CHAPTER TWELVE

Finding a System That's Right for You— What's a Viable Approach?

The first point to keep in mind when selecting a trading system is that there is no easy money to be made in the futures market. Public traders don't always believe that. Last year, I spoke at a systems seminar for people who wanted to learn a trading system. As I started to give a balanced portrayal of the pros and cons of trading systems and the pitfalls of futures trading, I suddenly became aware that a number of would-be speculators didn't believe that making money in the pit, let alone off the floor, was enormously difficult. It is tough work, so at the outset you have to disabuse yourself of the notion of easy money.

BEWARE THE CURVE-FITTED SYSTEM

It is very important to know how the system you are going to use was formed. A lot of systems are created by approaching a computer expert and saying, "Look, I'm interested in soybeans. I want you to develop a mathematical formula that will give me optimum results for buying and selling beans based on the experience of the past four or five years." The programmer instructs the computer to make millions of calculations from the data bank. When enough numbers are crunched you will have a system, but it probably will not be a very good one. A system should not be developed by taking the results and fitting a system around them. A better way is to design a system around an idea and see what kind of results you get.

Curve-fitting is nothing more than taking the desired results and finding a system that will yield those results. It means taking a trend-following method when the market is trending and a trading method when the market is trading narrowly. If you knew in advance what kind of market to expect, devising a system would be easy. Some methods work better during certain markets than others. The key is knowing which method to use in a particular market—and knowing when to switch as the market changes.

THE PITFALLS OF OPTIMIZATION

You have to be very careful about how your system was developed. Was it designed by computer optimization or around a market-tested idea? Even with good ideas you can have problems. In volatile markets, the assumptions often aren't valid. The system may fill you at every stop. Let's say you are short and you get stopped out. Will you get filled at the stop price? Chances are, under actual market conditions, this wouldn't be possible. Anyone who ever entered a stop order and saw the market shoot through it like a hot knife through butter, knows that the order could be filled 150 points away. So be on the lookout for similar false assumptions.

You also have to consider the time period on which the system was based. For example, it would be worthless to invest in a soybean system based on the years 1974-78 because beans were in a bull market then. Remember, there are a lot more contracts today than there were five years ago, when we didn't even have S&Ps. Obviously, S&Ps

have taken customers away from soybeans, thus cutting down on their volatility. In analyzing your system you must consider whether the volatility is the same today as it was four or five years ago when the system was first developed.

GOOD AND BAD ASSUMPTIONS

There are literally thousands of systems you can use, but you should look for one that you feel comfortable with and that can give you some guidelines.

You'd be surprised how many systems have bad assumptions. Is a system tested only in a period of rising prices going to work in a bear market, or a sideways market? Some systems base all their assumptions on a bull market. Take the S&Ps, for example. We really don't know yet what a bear market in the S&P is like because we've had a bull market since the S&Ps began trading in April 1982. Could we go to a 600-point discount in a bear market? We don't know. We haven't been there.

IDENTIFY YOUR MARKETS

Identify the markets you wish to trade. Depending upon whether you intend to be a long- or short-term trader, you should select just two or three commodities or futures out of a universe of perhaps thirty. Some systems, such as the Commodex system, trade many commodities, but you are better off concentrating on less than a handful of markets. They might be S&Ps, soybeans, cattle and Japanese yen.

Your next task will be to learn as much as you can about those markets. What are their fundamentals? What affects their price history? Do they have seasonal patterns? What can you learn from their long-term price charts? The point is, learn as much as you can about your markets.

You have to select contracts that have some liquidity. Obviously, you shouldn't pick flaxseed, tin or London rubber to trade because they aren't liquid enough. If it is day trading that interests you, you'll probably want to limit yourself to the two best day-trading vehicles: S&Ps and Treasury bonds. Ultimately, your selection will depend on your interests.

TEST YOUR SYSTEM

You'll want to test different systems on different markets. Ideally, you should test a system for three to five years. During that time you are likely to encounter a bull market, a bear market and a dead market. Then analyze the results.

In analyzing a day-trading method, you'll want to know how the system was developed. Was it tested on tick data or on open, high, low and close data? It makes a significant difference, especially when you are considering whether a specific signal was taken. Did the market actually trade at that price? If it didn't, chances are you will never do as well under actual trading conditions. If the proper research and development went into the systems you should get a fair return on your money.

The S&P market is becoming a very large day-trading market. You'll find that often the open interest may be only 60,000 contracts while the volume is 80,000 to 100,000 contracts. The disparity tells you that an awful lot of day trading is taking place. Because everyone in the pit knows that, technical considerations play an important role. The floor knows where the double tops and bottoms are, where the head and shoulders formations are and how to utilize that information. Locals usually have a good idea where the stops are. In developing a system, you want to take this kind of information into account. There can be an edge in taking the information right off the floor and coming up with a strategy real quick. The problem is, most people can't do it.

THE PERSONALITY OF THE MARKET

You won't find a cattle trader in the currency pits because each market has a distinct personality. They also behave differently in bull and bear markets. Thus, the gold market is different from the soybean market, which is different from the S&P market. Furthermore, *markets have a tendency to change over time.* That's why the 1980 gold market is nothing like the 1986 gold market. You have to evaluate the personality of the market you trade and select a system that is built around its unique traits.

The S&P market has a personality all its own. I like to think of it as a teenager—volatile and unpredictable. Compare this with the sleepy silver market of the last few years. Every market trades differently. You can't take rules that apply to Deutschemark futures and apply them to, say, S&P futures.

WHO CREATED THE SYSTEM?

Lastly, in evaluating a trading system, ask yourself the most pertinent question of all: Who created the system? I'd prefer to place my money on a professional who knows the market. Is the seller of the system in the business of selling trading systems or making money in the market? There is an enormous amount of money made on Wall Street these days. Unfortunately, many "experts" appearing in the media make their living *from* the market, not *in* the market. There is a difference.

ASK SOMEONE WHO'S DONE IT—NOT A SO-CALLED "EXPERT"

You don't go to the doctor and find out you have something wrong with your chest and go check it out with a real estate salesman. Why do you go to a doctor? Why do you go to a specialist? Not for easy answers, but for practical ones. In a corporation, the lower you go in the corporate hierarchy, the more readily available are the answers. The higher up you go, the less they know and the more willing they are to admit to it. It is the same thing here but just the opposite. The bank president is willing to admit he doesn't know anything about the economy. But the people down in the bookkeeping department have all the solutions to all the problems—from social security to why your husband is impotent. It's a little like George Burns' observation that it is too bad all the people who can solve our problems are driving cabs or cutting hair.

CHAPTER THIRTEEN

A Business, Not a Hobby

Trading is an entrepreneurial-type business—not a hobby. With enough time and effort, it is a business that will reward you well. Yet many investors treat trading in a casual fashion because they feel they can always go back to their "real" job if they fail. I'm in this game to win. I'm in it because I like the money, the freedom and the feeling of being rewarded right away when I take a risk and win.

NOTHING BETTER IN THE WORLD

If you are good at stock index futures trading, it can be the most gratifying profession in the world. The hours are reasonable, and I can take a vacation whenever I want to. Actually, I don't think of trading as work because to me beating the market is an exciting challenge. In the pit, nobody tells me what to do. I can make as much money as my skill and daring allow. Compare this to corporate life, where executives often wait years to receive the salary and recognition they deserve. For this reason alone, a corporation couldn't hold me—unless I owned it and could rise or fall on my own efforts. That's how it is in the futures game.

What's more, a corporation probably couldn't pay me enough to make it worth my while. Several years ago, when I was hot in the currency market, a West Coast bank approached me about a position as a currency trader. I dismissed the idea immediately when they told me that the salary was $80,000 a year. I was making five or six times as much on the floor, and I wasn't going to take a pay cut for the sake of job security.

THE ONLY THING THAT COUNTS: HOW GOOD ARE YOU?

When I worked in the banking and brokerage business, attitudes about "corporate policy" used to bother me. In one instance I was nearly fired over this issue.

I had sent a note to my clients advising them to sell a certain stock that happened to be on the firm's recommended list. Eight clients out of about 15 sold their holdings in response to my note. When the branch manager reviewed the week's buys and sells, he realized that I had contradicted the firm's recommendations. When he questioned my actions I told him I didn't care. The stock was overpriced. The point is, that's the kind of nonsense you have to put up with in the corporate world. You are often evaluated not on your performance, but on your willingness to follow the rules.

The futures market, on the other hand, rewards competence and punishes incompetence. The only thing that counts is how good you are. Unfortunately, many participants in the futures markets don't want to take the time to become competent. They don't take trading seriously; they treat it like a hobby. I know that most public customers have jobs, so trading is incidental. If they have several weeks of losses, they can go back to their jobs and forget about trading. What's surprising is that this indifference also exists down on the floor. There are traders who have paid $100,000 for an exchange membership acting as if they're just trying to find themselves. If you don't know who you are, the market's an expensive place to find out. Futures trading is my career, so you can bet I'm serious about what I'm doing.

A QUESTION OF SECURITY

In today's world, there is no such thing as security. Ask anyone who's been fired. As for retirement, I'm 35 years old. I don't want to go through life looking forward to the day when I'm 65. When I reach that age, I'll be financially self-reliant. But will those people who opted for security? In my opinion, the risk/reward ratio in corporate life is very poor. If you are good in the futures business, you can turn that ratio in your favor; if you are bad, you will be forced out before you lose more.

DEALING WITH FAILURE

A number of you may have tried and failed in the futures market. Welcome to the human race. So you lost. My definition of a loser is one who is afraid to fail. In the corporate world you are taught to avoid failure at all costs, whereas in this business the secret of success is learning *how to deal with failure*. Sooner or later, everyone loses in one way or another. It is *how* you lose that is important.

I've already mentioned that I fail a couple of hundred times a day. I make about 1,000 decisions a day, and I act on about 10 percent of them. A considerable percentage are wrong, but I don't have to be right all the time. My goal is simple: I just want to make money. I don't go crazy when a trade turns sour.

THE HOBBYIST VERSUS THE PROFESSIONAL

Professional traders know that money is important but, unlike hobbyists, they focus on the market. Professionals know that money is just a way to keep score, whereas customers who treat the market like a hobby have a hard time concentrating on anything *but* the money. When customers see the market go five, six or seven ticks against them, their reaction is: "It will come back. I've got it covered." By that time, most professionals would have taken the loss and left the market. But customers think differently. Even as the market continues to move against them, they buy more and dig themselves in deeper.

The unsuccessful ones are uncomfortable with profits but not with losses. The professionals, of course, are just the opposite. They know that if they can tame their losses the profits will take care of themselves.

When I was a broker, one of my firm's clients was a young couple who were trading currencies. They made money for eight consecutive days, taking nine or ten ticks out of the Japanese yen each day. On the ninth day the yen opened 50 higher, and they bought the first break. The yen soon collapsed, but instead of getting out at a loss, they decided to double up. The yen went limit down and they couldn't get out, so they made another fatal mistake: They spread the yen position against the Deutschemark, which wasn't limit down yet. The next day the Deutschemark was up 76 while the yen was down 92—so they got murdered on both legs of the position. That was the last time I ever saw them.

Stories like this illustrate what happens if you are not prepared for contingencies. You can't let the emotions of the moment tell you what to do, yet I see this irrational approach even on the trading floor, where members should know better. I remember an incident several years ago when the Dow was up about 16 points one morning. We had to stop trading because the computers were down in New York and we didn't have access to price quotes. Without thinking, a group of S&P traders rushed to the phones to buy Value Line contracts in Kansas City to hedge their short positions in the S&P. Treating these orders like any other customer orders, the Kansas City traders rallied the Value Line price about 100 points. With the computers out, no one realized that the Dow had begun to decline. When the market reopened, the Dow was up only about four points, which caused the Value Line to plummet about 200 points. The S&P traders who bought Value Line contracts were trapped. Another winning scheme had gone awry

FROM THEORY TO PRACTICE

Commitment and dedication determine who becomes a professional trader and who continues to treat the market as a hobby. Becoming skilled in the futures market is not much different from weight training. You can't expect to read a book by Arnold Schwarzenegger, pick up a few weights and look like a body-builder. By the same token, you can read the principles outlined in this book, but at some point you have to put them into practice. To make it in this business, you have to survive some horrendous hits; you have to level off your emotional peaks and valleys. It requires dedication.

When I first became interested in the futures markets, I spent countless hours studying the personalities of various markets, analyzing charts, reading books on technical analysis, listening to customers and trying to figure out why they lost money so often. I finally realized that all the study was meaningless unless I put it into practice. Hundreds of traders on the floor of the Merc have intricate charts and can tell you what the Japanese yen did on June 20, 1966. But they probably haven't made any money lately. Many of them don't have the confidence to strip away the emotion and step up to the plate. That's what it takes to make money at this demanding game.

MAKING A COMMITMENT

A lot of people will read this book and say, "I'd like to try earning a living as a trader." But do they really want to take the risk? How will their families react when they announce that they are leaving a secure job and will spend their life savings on a membership at the Chicago Mercantile Exchange? *Does success in the market mean that much?* It has to. Unless they are willing to make a full-time commitment to trading, these people ought to try something else. It doesn't make sense to come down to the floor to trade one-lots. Why take that kind of risk to make $30,000 a year?

Mental toughness and discipline are required to survive— let alone prosper—in the futures market. The road to success is rough and lonely. Most people quit along the way. Some people become over-confident after a few early successes. They think they are experts, but they don't realize that they might hit the top one day and crash the next. The emotional swings could destroy them, and when it does you hear the excuses: "I don't have time for it anymore." "I can't follow this anymore." "I'm confused." They haven't yet developed that mental toughness.

DON'T PAPER TRADE

I've said it before, but it bears repeating: *Don't ever paper trade.* Paper trading is a major pitfall of just about every new trader. When you paper trade, you can lose millions of dollars and not a single night's sleep. That's because it isn't actual money; it's a hypothetical loss. The false emotions and false sense of security you get from paper trading can hurt you if you decide to commit real funds in the market.

The only way to understand the market is to put your money down on the table. Do one-lot orders if that is all you can afford. It will probably cost you some money, but I guarantee that you will remember it. I've seen many people paper trade—down on the floor, in brokerage houses, in offices around the country—yet I've never seen anyone cross over from paper trading to real trading and make money. Why? Because when you paper trade, you don't experience the same emotions.

You're probably thinking, "You mean I should risk my money even when I don't know the markets?" That's exactly what I mean. If you want to learn from your mistakes, you have to put your money where your mouth is. You have to get used to dealing with your feelings when the market free-falls while you are long or skyrockets while you are short. You have to learn to fall back on your contingency plans.

CHAPTER FOURTEEN

How To Establish Your Trading Level

Before you begin to trade, you have to sit down and decide what kind of numbers you can do according to your capital base. Basically, the categories are as follows: one- to five-lots; five- to ten-lots; ten- to 20-lots; and over 20-lots. Those are the levels. Figure out what category you fall into, *stay* in that category a long time. As a general rule, a conservative trader will have at least $20,000 in margin for every contract traded. Many traders, especially those on the floor, tend to be undercapitalized. On the other hand, they have a few advantages, such as instant liquidity, that public speculators don't enjoy.

It is important that you have the correct tools going into the game. Do you have the money to trade S&P futures? If you don't, you are going to have a hard time doing the right things. So try to establish your capital base *before* you undertake your first trade.

STAYING POWER

You also need staying power. That's why I say you have to be prepared to trade your personal level a long time. If you are a one-lot trader, for instance, you can't start jumping up to ten contracts. I can guarantee that if you have ten winning one-lot trades, as soon as you hop up to the ten-lot level, you'll have a loss. And that ten-lot loss will wipe out the profits on the previous ten winners. You have to be aware of the psychological component. You think differently on a ten-lot trade than you do on a one-lot. So start out at a level you feel comfortable with and be prepared to stay with it.

Once you have managed to *significantly increase* your capital base, you can move your trading level upward. If you do, be prepared to stay with the higher numbers. You don't have to trade the same number on every trade, but you should stay within the same range. This will ensure that you have the wherewithal, both emotionally and financially, to stay in the game no matter what happens in the market.

This approach will give you the proper mental attitude. Otherwise, you are going to end up trading too much. If you are not prepared for it, increasing the frequency and the size of your trades is like climbing into an oven and turning it up to broil. You can make mistakes under pressure like that.

$20,000 IN MARGIN FOR EVERY ONE-LOT

As a rule, you, the public trader, should have at least $20,000 in margin for every one-lot. Otherwise, you'll become too concerned with random ticks. If you have a small-time perspective when the market is bullish, you can buy all day and still lose money. On a 50- or 60-point break, you will get frightened and sell before the bottom falls out; then, on the subsequent rally, you will go long again and the same thing will happen. You make mistakes like that because you are worried about the money. Keep enough money in your account so that you can concentrate on the important thing—the trade.

LEARN TO TAKE TRADING BREAKS

To become a successful trader, you must maintain a healthy mental attitude. That means being able to turn the market on and off. Don't think of trading breaks as time wasted, but as time invested in your success. Sure, you have to pay your dues down in the pit, but for your own well-being you should take regular breaks from the market. If you have made money on some trades and want to take some time off, do it! If you don't, you will get wrapped up in the market and become a 24-hour trading animal. There will always be an opportunity to make money, so don't worry about missing an active day.

THE TRADING ANIMAL SYNDROME

I've noticed that when some people become traders their personalities change. They tend to look at things in shorter and shorter time intervals. They begin taking price charts home in the evening. Instead of relaxing by watching television or playing with the kids, they spend their spare time analyzing charts and becoming obsessed with day-to-day market activity.

The next day, you are too tired and worried to concentrate on your job, so you call your broker and start trading like an animal. You buy and sell, going in and out of the market to pick up a few ticks. Pretty soon, it is costing you $20 a minute because of the commissions. And soon your $20,000 is gone.

THE STORY OF MAGIC—A LESSON IN CONFIDENCE

I remember a local who used to trade gold. His nickname was Magic—probably because he seemed to have the magic touch when it came to making money in the market. He managed to make a lot of money even though he did just about everything wrong. Sometimes he would bid and offer at the same price.

"Doesn't anyone in here want to take a chance?" he'd yell. "I'll buy 'em at a half or sell 'em at a half." Magic didn't care. He just wanted the action.

Well, he soon refined his system. Rather than letting just anyone decide whether he'd buy or sell, he'd flip a coin. Heads he'd buy, tails he'd sell. Simple system, right? You'd be surprised the success he had with it.

Part of Magic's system was to buy or sell early in the day and then go downstairs to the bar. At around one o'clock in the afternoon he would come back upstairs and exit his position. The amazing thing about him was his willingness to sell into even the biggest bull market in history. Even though the gold market had risen to over $800 an ounce, if the coin came up tails he'd sell 50 contracts and go downstairs to the bar. This went on for about six months. He'd be wrong occasionally, but he never lost much money. The pit traders would eagerly await his flip of the coin every morning. Most locals would take home charts to study the fundamentals of the market, but Magic would just flip a coin and come up a winner. His method seemed to work like magic.

I remember the day he came in drunk. The market was screaming upward and his flip came up tails. He didn't care. He sold 50 cars and headed back to the bar. As soon as he left the pit, the gold market went about $30 higher.

"Should we send someone downstairs to tell Magic?" one local asked. "He might not like this price action." We couldn't believe he'd stay short 50 contracts through this bull move. It was obvious that his luck had run out.

At about ten minutes to one, Magic stumbled back into the pit. Just as he arrived the gold market broke on some news. It was off about $45 an ounce in 10 minutes. That's $10 or $15 *below* where Magic sold his 50 cars.

Naturally, Magic had already bought back his 50 cars.

"But weren't you worried when it rallied against you?" one of the locals asked.

"When?" Magic asked. "What are you talking about?

You saw me. I just bought them back fifteen bucks below where I sold them."

We told him to look at the high of the day posted up on the boards.

"Oh." He was sobered. "Well I made a profit, didn't I?"

The moral of this story is that sometimes you are better off not watching the market. Also, since this system obviously had no merit, it illustrates that luck plays a role. But ultimately Magic began to believe in his own magic. He thought he was invincible. That's when his trouble began. In August 1982, at the beginning of the big bull market, he began trading S&P futures. He got short a couple hundred contracts and went bankrupt. He was forced out of the market.

I remember the situation very well. Bonds, bills, currencies—all the financials were limit up, and the S&Ps were crawling higher. He had plenty of opportunity to get out of his position. The market had gone only about 50 to 100 points against him so far, but that last hour did him in. From two to three o'clock, the S&Ps were 500 points higher. To compound his problem, he sold more on the rally, trying to average the loss. The next day the market opened another 300 higher. He lost a fortune.

That's what happens when you violate so many rules. Magic took too many contracts, and he didn't get out when he had the opportunity. His notion that he was invincible finally killed the guy.

THE SURE-THING TRADE

You will eventually want to increase your trading level to capture a good move. How will you know when that time has come? I would say that about 99 percent of the time volatility will be the key. After I've spotted one of these good moves and made money by loading up on the correct side, other traders have asked me to explain "How I foresaw the move." "Why did you stand there with your arms crossed when it initially rallied 200 points? And how did you know when to get in?" I'll tell you a secret: I really didn't see the initial move coming, I knew what to look for and how to "read" the market. It is as simple as that. Volatility will tell you where the market wants to go. Once you know the direction, you can wait for the inevitable reaction. Then you go for it.

CHAPTER FIFTEEN ─────────

─────────────────

Should You Speculate?

To be a successful futures trader requires a certain kind of temperament. Now there are certain rules, such as the one that tells you to look for changes in the market, that you'll want to follow. But there are others that are directly dependent on your temperament toward risk. They don't need a lot of discussion and they are not rules you are going to find in other books. But they are important. One of them goes to the heart of the problem: Should you indeed speculate? This, after all, is a philosophical question that only you can answer.

Most texts outline how you should have a house, insurance, medical plans and a pension fund before you approach the futures market. Such advice is really useless. Obviously, if you are a shooter and the market is in your blood, who am I to tell you whether to speculate? This is a personal decision—one that only you can make. You can, if you wish, mortgage your house to trade futures. What right do I have to tell you not to? I borrowed every cent I could get my hands on and risked the wrath of my family to get in this business. Who am I to say that you shouldn't do the same? I can't do that. It is probably the logical thing to say, but it is not my place to say it. It depends on what kind of blood you have. If the game is in your blood, you have to go for it.

There's a sort of generation gap involved in one's temperament toward risk. Part of the decision to speculate has to do with your environment early in life. Being in my mid-thirties now, I spent the late 1960s and early 1970s as a teenager. As a result, for a significant portion of my adult life, I've known nothing but chaos in the world and in the market. Just in the past ten to 15 years, we'd had the gold standard repealed, the Vietnam war, the OPEC disaster, Watergate and a host of other market-moving events. So for people of my generation, we don't know anything but chaos and controversy. It is part of everyday life. The markets, of course, reflect this turmoil. So by the time the press gets hold of a story, such as the "Casino Society," you wonder where they've been all these years. The popularity of the new options and futures is nothing more than the market's way of dealing with all this risk we've grown so accustomed to. We are, in fact, finding better ways to manage risk and transfer it to people who are willing to accept it. I think the acceptance of these new products is an acceptance of the need to control an environment. It requires a certain perspective that many people on Wall Street have today.

Now an older person might have a slightly different attitude toward risk. Chances are an older person can remember back to a time when things were relatively calm. I remember somebody telling me once that the year I was born the bellwether government bond moved a point and a half the entire year. Today a move of that magnitude occurs everyday. And nobody even thinks about it. So the volatility is great today compared to years ago. This is especially true in the currency and stock markets. As a result, you have a whole generation of people, like myself, who are accustomed to dealing with risk. We've seen so many controversial events in our lifetime that we have grown used to markets skyrocketing and falling through the floor on a daily basis. So against this background, you have to consider someone who comes along and wants to trade S&Ps with $10,000 in his or her account. You can easily lose that kind of money in an afternoon. Yet, nobody told him or her that when he or she ventured into the market.

STOCK INDEX FUTURES TRADING IS A SPECIALTY

The investment game is different today. Thirty years ago, an investor had the alternative of putting his or her money in the stock market or in a savings account. Today we have more investment alternatives than we can count. This, of course, has given rise to a lot of specialties. Mine is trading the S&P market. So you can imagine my amazement when someone comes along with no background and no training in this field who wants to bet against me at my profession. The market demands a certain perspective and a novice or seasoned trader should try to cultivate that perspective.

You have to remember the basic fundamentals of the market: There is a loser for every winner, for instance. So if you are going to make money, you are going to take it out of someone's pocket. And the odds are that you will be taking it away from the professionals, who, I can assure you, hate to lose. You have to remember that every order has to flow through the pit. So when the customers make money, the professionals tend to lose it, and vice versa. So my question is this: What makes you think you should be able to do that? Think about it. And try to keep this perspective when you head to the bank to get a loan to trade S&Ps. There are no "can't-miss" trades. You can miss and you may be out a lot of money. Also, you have to remember that no matter how stressful the market becomes, there are people who can take both the risk and the stress. And it has no adverse effect on them. That's because they've grown accustomed to dealing with this high-risk game.

DEALING WITH FEAR AND GREED

Sometimes the classic market emotions of fear and greed can help you in the market, but not often. I'm reminded of my first big bond play in the market which gave me the money to move to the Merc. Essentially, it was a fear play which I used to my own advantage. It was during the period when interest rates were approaching their all-time high, near 21 or 22 percent—rates comparable to what the Mafia charges. I call it a "fear play" because, I reasoned, if rates didn't decline soon, the economy would be in chaos and the game, in more ways than one, would indeed be over. So, in looking back, I realized if rates were to rise still further, the country would be in very serious trouble. So what really was the risk since it wouldn't make any difference anyway? I was just terrified at the time and I decided to bet on lower rates. Fortunately, it paid off handsomely and I was able to parlay my winnings into a sizable amount.

Fear, however, often plays a more detrimental role in the marketplace. If, for instance, you fear for your life, you are going to act differently than if you are not fearful. So you have to be able to control the fear.

On the other side of the coin, you need to control the greed you feel on a trade. The way to do this is by saying, "I don't care about the money." And repeat it over and over again. This is really important. That's because if you look at any of the real successful traders in the futures market, you'll find that they've all mastered their control over their greed. To them, the money is truly meaningless in the sense that it doesn't influence their trading. That is, it is the trade that controls their actions. So they might indeed make ten million dollars in the market and they won't get out because of the money. Rather, they will only get out when the market tells them to get out. As a result, they will never get in a trade saying, "This is the one that will put me over the top." No way. That is pure and simple greed. Either a trade is good or it is bad. Period. *If it is bad, the rule is to cut it; if it is good, the rule is to stay until the market tells you otherwise.* And, if they happen to make a few million dollars on the good trade, so much the better.

Novice traders, on the other hand, tend to take the opposite attitude. They will take a trade determined to make a certain amount of money. So every tick up or down is so many dollars. Imagine what it must be like trying to make a milllion dollars on a trade and, having reached, let's say, $970,000, you hold out for the last $30,000—and you give it all back waiting the last $30,000? It happens. Why? Because some traders, but especially customers, tend to get tied in with their greed and forget about what the market is telling them to do.

PART 3

Strategies for Success

CHAPTER SIXTEEN _____

The Doubling Up Strategy

Two of the most important strategies in the market are *doubling up* and *doubling up and reversing*. Doubling up means taking more contracts. If the market moves against you, you might double up on your initial position by buying or selling additional contracts. Doubling up relies on the idea of a range, or resistance area, where you can add to your position with relative safety. Once outside this safety area, you will have to double up and reverse.

You can't simply take the rules for doubling up in the S&Ps and apply them to other markets. In the volatile S&P market, you can get away with more doubling up than in other markets, such as grains or meats. Whereas weather factors can create several bull and bear soybean markets within two years, chances are the amount of rainfall in the Midwest growing region won't move the financials one iota. The S&P market, by contrast, might move in one broad up or down trend that isn't hard to figure out except when the trend changes.

Whether to double up on the long or short side of the market depends on the trend. In a bull market, the odds favor making money when you double up on the long side; in a bear market, the odds favor the short side. The probabilities favor doubling up in a bull market by purchasing contracts and doubling up in a bear market by selling contracts.

As a floor trader, I tend to double up more than an off-the-floor trader because I have instant liquidity. With immediate market information and minimal transaction costs, I can turn around in a hurry. But the public trader paying commissions has to deal with the expense of trading.

Public traders tend to pick too narrow a range in which to double up. A 20-point difference in the S&Ps is meaningless. The key to getting ahead when you double up is to look for the inevitable bounce, or reaction. If you are buying and the market moves against you, the idea is to buy more and then get out on the bounce.

Let's say you buy at 90. If you double up and buy at 70, the range will be too narrow. But if you buy the quarters on the way down and sell them all on the rally back to 60, you'll be able to pay commissions and perhaps make a slight profit. Remember, though, that *when you double up, you aren't looking for profits; you are trying to emerge from a losing trade without serious damage.* Once your doubling up has gotten you out of trouble, you can start over again in a fresh state of mind.

Where to double up is a judgment call, not a mechanical reaction. One rule is based on volatility: *How good an area is for doubling up is determined by how fast it was created.* For example, let's say you are long and buy the market at 90. Over a two-hour period it trades down to 55, creating a 35-point range. You know you can buy at 55, because the locals did everything in their power to take the market lower and couldn't do it. The only way they could take it down would be by selling contracts, so overall, they have to be short. Implicit in this situation is a potential for an explosive upward move. In this situation you want to be a buyer. The market will probably rally, and when it does, you can get out.

When the market takes a long time to establish a range, there will be good support at the bottom and good resistance at the top of the range. In those areas short-term scalping provides buying and selling. The strategy, therefore, should be to buy at the bottom end of the range and sell near the top end. This can usually be accomplished without much risk.

But what if the market trades at 90 and falls to the lower quarter in 30 seconds? In this case, it would not be a good idea to double up yet. You want some tangible sign of support before you buy additional contracts. When you are long and the market breaks rapidly, watch out! The break may not be over.

This occurred on a recent Monday when the Dow closed the day 45 points lower. I made a lot of money that day, but I could have made much more. Here's what happened.

I came in bullish on the day. The bonds were up ten points when the S&P market opened, so I was expecting a nice rally. Instead, the S&P market was down 50 points at the open on extremely aggressive commercial selling. Then it fell another 75 points almost immediately. Something didn't make sense: The bonds were strong, but the commercials were selling the S&Ps as fast as they could. Sensing a bottom, I bought S&P contracts and the bonds immediately rallied another ten points. In the S&P pit, however, the market was static. Every time the locals tried to rally the S&Ps, the commercials and commission houses would come in with big sell orders.

An hour into the trading session I was long about 20 cars and the market was trading two or three ticks against me. I wasn't in deep trouble yet, but I knew I would be if the bonds were to break. What's more, if the bonds rallied and the commercials and commission houses kept selling, the market would probably break. The bonds maintained their 20-point gain on the day, but the S&Ps began to slip.

Then the bonds broke, and the S&Ps slipped even more. That's when I decided to double up and buy another 20 contracts. I was going with the bond trend, which had been strong all morning.

After doubling up, I was long my initial 20 contracts, which I bought at around 60, and an additional 20, which I bought at 25. I was planning to close out these positions and start over as soon as the bonds rallied again, but that didn't happen. Instead, the bonds finished down on the day, two full basis points. Even when the bonds reached their high, the S&Ps didn't budge. My attempt to average the loss wasn't working.

How was I to get out of my 40 cars without disturbing the market? I knew I couldn't take a chance on bluffing the market. If I began to bid big on size to spook a few locals, I'd run the risk of being picked off.

The pop that usually enables me to sell my contracts had not materialized. I realized that I'd made a mistake in doubling up. Most markets, including the S&P, will give you an opportunity to double up and get out alive if you follow one basic principle: Exit the position when you break even. On this day, I didn't get that opportunity. Fortunately, after recognizing my mistake I was able to get short in a serious way and make a substantial amount of money.

Once you double up and get out, does that mean you have to reverse positions? Not at all. If you are initially a buyer, it doesn't mean you won't get bullish again. The purpose of getting out by doubling up is to improve your frame of mind. Obviously, when you bought the first group, you made a mistake. Take the opportunity to scratch the trade and start over.

DOUBLING UP AND REVERSING

If you double up too soon and the market plummets, you might be left holding contracts you bought near the highs.

When this happens, your only recourse is to look for a rally and then double up and reverse. Don't try to place limit orders to reverse. You won't have that luxury at this point. Just go retail and sell everything at the market.

Doubling up and reversing is one of the hardest strategies to implement because you have to know what separates a random tick from a price direction change. When the market rallies to new high ground and then backs off 30 points, is that the start of a big correction—one from which the market will fall another 200 points? Or is that 30-point dropoff just a reflection of profit-taking? With those sellers leaving the market, will it rally another 50? Is this break the start of something big, meaning I should start selling aggressively? The answers to questions like these are judgment calls. Despite the difficulty of making such judgments, there are clues you can follow.

Watch the Price Action

A lot of price action near a day's high often indicates just the running of the stops. Sensing resting orders just above the day's high, locals will frequently bid the market up to precipitate a market rally. What's driving the market—size or small orders? You don't always have access to this kind of information on the outside, but it helps to have some idea of the quality of the buying and selling.

Follow the Players

You can often assess the quality of the move by what the locals and commercials are doing. If, for example, a rally is totally inspired by the locals and you are short, you can usually get away with fading the rally. Chances are, the locals just don't have the staying power. The rally will probably end in a few minutes, and you can cover any short sales.

However, if both you and the pit are short and the rally is driven by the commercials buying, your attempt to double up by selling more will only result in additional losses. As a rule, when the commercials come in as big buyers, the rally has a long way to go.

Read the Volume

Doubling up and reversing is a judgment call that works most of the time. But when it doesn't work, it can clean you out. The volume in the stock market is the key to reversing. Say you have been short all morning and the market has continued to move against you. The Dow rallied a half point every 20 minutes and by noon it is up 13 points. The range in the nearby S&P futures is 180 points, but there hasn't been more than a 3- or 4-tick break all day. At this point, you have to look at the volume. If 100 million shares have traded by noon, the market isn't going to break. So you have an opportunity to reverse with the hope that the market will explode in the afternoon. However, if the volume is light and you reverse, you could lose a lot of money.

Assess the Volatility

As the volatility increases, so does the opportunity to double up and reverse. Volatility is a function of price: The market becomes more volatile as it goes higher. If the Dow ever reaches 3,000, you can expect 1,000-point ranges everyday. That's when doubling up and reversing will work best.

CHAPTER SEVENTEEN

The Tripling Up Strategy

Tripling up involves taking a third level. Because you are adding to a loser, the strategy is psychologically difficult. When the strategy works—and it will about 90 percent of the time—count yourself fortunate, get out of the market and start over again. It takes judgment and skill to execute this risky strategy, so unless you have progressed from a novice to an intermediate futures trader, you better not attempt it. There is no magic number that will tell you where to triple up. You can't just triple up 50 points below your previous entry. It isn't that simple.

Why triple up? Simply put, to make a last-ditch effort to salvage a trade. There are two rules you absolutely *must* follow with this strategy:

1. Liquidate every position *immediately* if, after tripling up, the market moves even a modest amount against you.
2. Take *more positions* on the third and final entry level.

There's a good reason for both rules. Let's say you are long one contract. The market falls 100 points, so you double up and buy another. Then it drops another 20 points and you buy *two* more contracts. You are taking twice as many at the third level because you want your base to be larger than the trades you took on at a higher level. What began as a simple one-lot trade has now become a four-lot trade. The secret is that *you must liquidate the entire position if the market moves just one or two ticks against you.* Thus, the final entry must be the bottom—or you exit the market. Unless you exercise enormous discipline, you will find yourself in real difficulty. With a close stop, that extra contract on the final entry won't really hurt you if you are wrong, but it may be your salvation if you are correct.

Let me illustrate how I put this strategy to work one Friday afternoon about an hour before the close. The market was down from its highs and I had been short, so I already made my money for the day. I decided to limit myself to one- and two-lot trades because I didn't want to jeopardize my profits. The market had been up $15 over the previous day's close. After the break, it was up only about $7, so I figured it was time to take a position on the long side. I didn't think it would close lower on the day because the S&Ps were already 300 points off the high. The locals had to be short. When they tried to cover their positions at the first sign of strength they would provide me with the bounce I was looking for.

First I bought a couple of cars at 231.80, but the market immediately dropped to 231.50. When the market fell to 231.25, I purchased two more contracts. Altogether, I was long four contracts.

The locals were becoming more and more bearish. I realized that their selling would add fuel to the fire if they had to come in as buyers on a short-covering rally. Given the overwhelming bearishness of the pit, I bought another six contracts as soon as the market traded down to 231 even. What started as a two-lot trade had suddenly become a ten-lot trade, and the market was still moving against me.

This position was getting too serious for a Friday afternoon. So, because my expensive contracts were higher up and I didn't have very many of them, I decided to bend the rules and take a fourth level position. I resolved, however, to abide by the spirit of the rule, if not the letter: When the market hit 80, I bought ten more contracts. But if it touched 70, I would liquidate the entire position. I was risking just two ticks on the final ten contracts. Then, one car traded at 75. As I was about to offer my 20 cars at a price of 70, there was a 95 bid on 300 cars. I couldn't believe it. We were about to collapse and the buyers came rushing into the market. The short sellers panicked. Within 20 seconds, we were at the higher 45, where I immediately sold my 20 contracts. In all, I made $4,000 on that trade.

Looking back, I had no business making money on that position. I was able to apply the secrets of doubling and tripling up successfully because:

- I knew what I wanted to risk.
- I bought the most contracts at the lowest level, where I could sell them most quickly.

Had the market hit 70 or lower, I would have hit the next lower bid on all 20 cars. I wouldn't have lost much because only four contracts were for more than 80. That's the secret of doubling and tripling up. Even when you have to take a chance on a fourth level, ask yourself: Where do I double up? What levels do I use? How far apart am I willing to let it go? And at what point do I quit?

This strategy usually works, but when it doesn't it costs money. When I lose money with this strategy, which is not often, it's because I get whipsawed by the market. This means that I buy only to see the market decline, and then I sell just prior to a rally. Such whipsawing price action can get quite expensive. Remember, though, that even on ranges of about 500 points, I am risking only a tick or two. You have to use this strategy based on probabilities. Once you have developed your trading to an art, you'll know when to double and triple up and when not to.

The only hard-and-fast rule is that you can only double or triple up a couple of times before you have to make the decision to blow out of the trade.

LEARN HOW TO READ THE MARKET

If you know what to look for, the market will usually tell you where it wants to go. For instance, let's say you purchase an S&P contract and the market breaks 200 points. The market is telling you that it is serious about going lower. So on the next rally you have to take aggressive action—first by selling out the long positions and then by selling short. The market broke because there are a lot of people who want to sell. To use this strategy, you need ready access to a quote machine or you won't be able to take action effectively. But once you see that sign, you have to act.

REVERSING

You have to be patient when you reverse. When I'm about to reverse positions, I look at what other key markets, especially the bonds and key stocks such as IBM, are doing. You want to find several indicators that point in the same direction.

One day, when the Dow dropped 45 points, I started off the day long. The selling signals soon became evident. The bonds started the day strong but turned weak and went limit down. At that point the big stocks, such as IBM and General Motors, also began to weaken. Pretty soon, the S&Ps couldn't rally at all. From an initial bullish stance, I became a heavy seller. In the S&P market, the normal follow-through is for bonds to be strong and for the stock market to rally. When that pattern doesn't occur, it's a sign that something is wrong.

HOW TO READ THE VOLUME

Volume is another important indicator to look for prior to reversing. In a bull market, you don't want a big break or a big rally on light trading. In fact, the big moves will almost always occur on heavy volume. The size of your position should be dictated by volume. Save a big order for the day when the volume is heavy. It doesn't have to reach record levels, but it should be strong enough to suggest a nice rally later in the afternoon. For instance, if the market is up and rallies on a volume of 130 million shares traded in New York by noon, that's a signal to load up. The market is telling you that it is going much higher.

Light volume can mean trouble. If the trend has been up but the Dow drops ten points or more in the first hour on light volume, perhaps 20 million shares, you have to become an aggressive buyer. A decline on weak volume suggests a shallow move. On these days, the bullish signal is so clear that I may double, triple and even quadruple up. That's because 99 times out of 100 when the weak volume disappears, the buying will increase again and the market will head higher. When you know what to look for, volume can be a pretty reliable indicator.

MAKING JUDGMENTS

Volatility, volume, other markets, key stocks—these are the clues that can help you form an opinion on the market. The professionals spend their careers learning how to read these clues, so don't be concerned if it takes time to learn how to spot the signals. If you can't watch the market and interpret the clues for yourself, you probably should not try sophisticated strategies like doubling up and reversing.

If you are long and you see a 100-point break and no up-ticks, be thankful that the market has tipped its hand—then act! Take the loss on the rally; then load up on the downside. Do not buy more because the market has suddenly become a bargain. It hasn't. Instead, on the next rally of 20 to 25 points, go "retail" and get out at the market. With any luck, you will have a little up-spike in the market. Then the true downward trend will reemerge and the bottom will fall out. Once the break occurs, it will be too late to do anything about it.

When a market suddenly weakens, many traders ignore the warning signs. They rationalize that it must have broken because there weren't enough buy orders or because the traders in New York were asleep. Then, when a rally does occur, they become overly optimistic. But they are wrong. If anything, the market is weak. After all, it broke 100 points but rallied only 20.

If you want to know where the bottom will occur following one of these disastrous blowouts to the downside, you only have to watch for these uninformed buyers to come into the market as sellers. When the buyers throw in the towel, you've probably seen the low of the move. That, by the way, is where experience counts. The professionals wait for the signs and then risk their money on trades that have the probabilities behind them. They let the market tell them what to do.

CHAPTER EIGHTEEN ─────────

───────────────────

The Lumber Story

There's a lot of talk about floor locals muscling markets. And most of it is just that—talk. The locals might get the S&P market to move a little faster or a little slower for a second or two, but their impact is very slight because there's so much liquidity and so much diversity of opinion in this market. Prices are more likely to fluctuate in less liquid markets.

To illustrate how this lack of liquidity allows some traders to play games with prices, let me tell you what happened to me in the lumber market. A lot of people on the floor make serious money in lumber. When lumber runs, it is a perfect market—like beans in a drought—you buy it and it goes to the moon.

I watched the lumber market for a while and decided to get in when it went down to about $125 per board foot. I went to my clearing firm's trading desk on the floor and I told them to buy me two July lumber contracts at a dollar and a half below the current market price. If the order got hit, fine; if not, who cares? I soon forgot about the order, but when I looked up at the board awhile later I saw that lumber had traded down to my buy price and through it by 30 or 40 cents. The next time I looked, it had rallied about $4.

A lot of lumber traders on the floor are position traders who hold their positions for weeks, perhaps even months. I don't believe in staying in the market for long, so I put in an order to sell a little above the high of the day, at even money. The next rally, around noon, didn't quite reach that level. I decided to walk into the lumber pit and create a little havoc. The locals knew I was a large S&P trader, so they were immediately skeptical.

When I bid 20 on 20 contracts, all hell broke loose. Nobody would hit me. The whole pit started bidding and the price shot up to 80. My *sell* order was just a little higher, at even. As I had expected, no one was willing to sell me any lumber. I was bidding, they were bidding and lumber prices were climbing steadily. I was just trying to bluff them into bidding it up. I knew no one would hit me. No one in that pit hits anyone because they are all edge traders *par excellence*. Give them the edge and you might have a trade.

MY BLUFF WORKS

When I bid 20 on 20 contracts, the reaction was predictable. The locals assumed that I wouldn't want to buy 20 contracts unless I was certain prices were headed higher, so a few of them took it up to 80 bid. Then, to have a little fun with them, I bid 90. Sure enough, they immediately bid it higher! Finally, one of the locals asked me how many I was planning to buy.

"I don't know," I replied. "Maybe a hundred and fifty."

He then bid right through my sell price, and I saw the broker with my order sell him a couple. Somebody else then bid ten. Then 20. It was on the high of the day. Sell orders soon began pouring into the pit, and the market broke about 300 points in the last 45 minutes of trading. But I didn't care. I was already out with a profit.

In looking back on my lumber episode, I realize that I didn't buy a single contract that day. That's the way thinly traded commodities like lumber work. When you bid, the pit goes to the next highest offer. If you want to buy at 70, the pit traders will sell to you at 80. If you want to buy at 80, they'll let you buy at 90. That's edge trading. If you want to buy at 60 in the S&P market, chances are someone will sell it to you there. Differences of opinion, after all, make the market. But the lumber traders thought they could make me pay up to get in the market. Little did they know that I was already long and just wanted to sell my two contracts.

I learned an important lesson from this experience: *Never day trade a thin market.* If *I* can push a market around, so can someone else—and I don't want it pushed against me.

YOU NEVER REALLY KNOW WHAT ANYONE IS DOING

Although a lot of smaller traders like to follow on the heels of the larger traders, you never know what anyone is doing in the pit. My excursion into the lumber pit convinced me of that. When a floor trader is buying or selling, how can the locals judge whether that trader is already long or short, or whether he has a position or not? Unless the trader tells them—and few will—they won't know. A lot of traders fill public orders in addition to trading for their own accounts. They might be day trading, position trading or simply scalping a tick or two. The bigger traders will bluff to spook the smaller traders.

There's a story about a big trader in pork bellies, who, while offering to sell contracts all the way up in a sustained bull market, had his broker quietly buying contracts across the pit. When he saw the broker buying 20s he sold 40s. When the broker bought 40s, he sold 50s. He must have sold between 200 and 300 contracts. The other pit traders thought he was getting killed. In fact, he was making money. The point is, you really can't be too concerned about what others are doing because even the most successful traders have losing streaks.

In the S&P market, where you have the locals, commission houses, commercials and arbs all fighting it out, it can be very unproductive to follow the larger traders. For one, the commercials have cash ties to the market. Chances are they just bought several million dollars worth of stocks and are selling S&Ps because they think the premium of futures over cash is too high. This sophisticated strategy, known as *program trading*, virtually assures the commercials of a profit. For a small five- or ten-lot trader to turn bearish based on program selling could be suicidal. The commercials don't care where the market goes because they don't have to get out of their positions like the small traders do. The same can be said of the arbs. With millions of dollars at their disposal, the arbs will pick up a tick or two by buying one market and selling another, if they can. If you are looking at just one market and following in their footsteps, you could be in trouble. Then, again, the big traders might intentionally bid on hundreds of contracts just to get the attention of the pit. Of course, someone could come in and sell them the contracts, but that's a risk they are willing to take. More often than not, the bluff works and they create mass confusion in the pit. It's all part of the game. As a big local, I sometimes do the same thing to get the market moving the way I want.

A LOCAL'S REPUTATION

That day in the lumber pit illustrates another important point: A local's reputation can bail him or her out of a jam. If a new trader had entered the lumber pit and bid on a one-lot, the regulars would have either ignored the bid or jacked it up. Then, as soon as the trader said a word about buying, they would have pounced on the trade. Traders know that their reputations precede them on the floor. They know who to take seriously and who to disregard, who has the money to take a 50-lot trade and who doesn't.

I can sometimes push the S&P market. If I start bidding it up and it really wants to skyrocket, it will just blow out of sight that much faster. But unlike the thin lumber market, the S&P can't be pushed where it doesn't want to go. The locals who have tried to do so have lost big.

USING SIZE TO INTIMIDATE

Much of what goes on in the pit is based on fear and intimidation. The public trader must wonder why a market that was a quarter bid a minute ago is now trading 100 points higher. Did some news hit the market? Why do prices change so suddenly? I'll tell you why: Not only is the market emotional, but you never know who might be working to outsmart the pit.

When large locals bid or offer on size, they may influence the pit. Let's say a broker gets an order to sell ten contracts at the market. If the market is currently 35 bid and 40 offered, the broker will try and sell the 40s. It is only logical to try for the best price. My strategy, like many others who use this technique, is to outsmart the pit into thinking the market is going lower. So, to generate some bearish sentiment, I might offer to sell 50 cars at 40. Not wanting to risk getting a bad fill in a 35-bid, 40-asked market, the broker will quickly sell ten at 35. That's when I'll buy. He might be surprised to see me reverse my position, but he has no choice. He has to sell them to me. Minutes later, perhaps even before the fill makes its way back to the originating brokerage office, prices may have risen and the customer will want to know why he or she got such a bad fill.

The same strategy works in reverse on the upside: I might bid up the market when I really want to sell. The element of surprise is essential. Before the locals realize what is happening, they have bought or sold ten or 20 contracts—and I have the position I wanted at a good price.

Ironically, a bad fill is usually a sign that you are right on the market. Remember, futures trading is very competitive. Floor traders are not in business to give good deals to the public—if anything, the opposite is true. We'll talk more about fills later.

Market Indicators

If you want to make money trading S&P futures, pay attention to the same indicators that the floor traders watch. Although you never know for sure which indicators will be pulling the strings, the key ones to watch are:

- IBM stock
- Treasury bond futures
- The Dow Jones transportation averages
- The Dow Jones industrials
- The ticks (number of stocks on up-ticks versus number on down ticks)
- The S&P cash index

Almost everyone on the floor watches IBM. That's why the S&P futures often move a fraction or so ahead of the S&P cash index, which is updated every minute. By watching IBM, the floor traders know whether the next published cash index price will be higher or lower. What's amazing is not the correlation of IBM to the S&P index or the Dow Jones industrials, but their occasional divergence—the index going one way and IBM another.

You'd be surprised how good a leading indicator the transports can be, especially in conjunction with the industrials. The strength or weakness in the transportation averages often unmasks an underlying trend that hasn't been reflected in the Dow Jones industrials yet. For example, if you find that the industrials are up 15 points and the transportation index is off a half point, look for a break in prices—something is up. The industrials won't usually be very strong when the transportation index is very weak. So you won't have the industrials up 30 with the transports down a half. When you do have a discrepancy in the two, the divergence pinpoints strength or weakness—generally in the direction of the transportation index.

This is not to say that the transportation average won't occasionally lag behind the industrials. If the industrials are strong, it may be only a matter of time before the other index follows suit. But if the transportation index can't follow, chances are the market wants to go the other way.

There's another reason to watch the transportation averages. Whereas the Dow Jones industrials will frequently jump back and forth between positive and negative, the transportation averages tend to open and go one way. So the trend tends to be truer. One way to capitalize on this tendency is to find a divergence in the two and follow the transportation index. Let's say the Dow Jones industrials are up four points and the transportation averages are down seven. The thinking might be that there isn't much left in the industrials, so the floor starts selling. Whereas the public customer watching a video screen might think that the industrials are strong and start buying, the floor is selling. Clearly, this is one divergence it pays to watch.

This rule is not a surefire way to beat the market. When the industrials are up seven points and the transportation averages are down seven points all day, you get total confusion. On days like that, the locals end up killing themselves because this particular indicator just doesn't work very well.

Obviously it would be easier if someone could issue a scorecard every day that said: "Today, we'll watch the bonds." On some days the bonds will lead the market, but on others they will be useless as an indicator. We recently had a day when the bonds were almost limit up and the Dow couldn't rally more than three and a half points. There was no price leadership in the bonds at all. So each time the bonds rallied, the locals bought the S&Ps. The commercials would then come in and crush them. When the bonds backed off, the market cracked because everyone was using that as an excuse to sell. So the locals bought all day to no avail—the S&P market just didn't want to rally. But who can say which indicator to watch on a given day? The next time the bonds rally, the S&P might rally 500 points.

WHICH IS THE BEST INDICATOR?

A lot of locals watch tick changes because they will change before the averages. So the Dow could be going up and the ticks will be +100, +200, +500, +600 and so on. Then, while the Dow is still rallying, you'll see the ticks start to regress, like: +485, +300, +185, −83. That's the sign that the Dow has peaked. The locals will see that pattern and start selling in anticipation of a break.

The locals really get confused when something happens that isn't supposed to happen. For example, I've already mentioned that the locals on the floor watch IBM for its price leadership. But many times the industrials will be up seven or eight dollars and IBM will be down two dollars. When the blue chips show this kind of divergence from the Dow, the locals don't know what to make of it.

Watch the Commercials

A good way to decide which indicator to watch is to observe which one the commercials are following. For instance, if the bonds rally and the commercials start buying them, the bonds are probably the indicator to watch that day. On the other hand, if the bonds rally and the commercials come in and crush the market, perhaps bonds are *not* the indicator to watch. When you are off the floor, you can't always tell what the commercials are doing, so you'll have to learn to read the tape to know what to look for. Let's set up a typical scenario.

Say the bonds are at 17 and the high of the day is 22. All of a sudden, the bonds rally from 17 to 28, taking out the high. Chances are the S&Ps will follow suit and rally along with the bonds. But what will happen when the bonds back off from 28 to 25? Will the S&Ps break by one or two ticks or will they break by ten? It makes a big difference. If the S&Ps break ten ticks, the commercials are giving the locals all they want and more. The market is now bearish. But if the S&Ps break only one or two ticks, it suggests strength, and the next move will likely be higher.

When you have the ten-tick break, all the locals will be long. At first they'll be looking for new buyers. But once the locals realize that there won't be any new buyers, they will head for the exit all at the same time, precipitating a sharp price break.

Good support in the above scenario suggests that the bonds are providing the price leadership. Hence, when they trade back to 28 or higher in the above example, the S&Ps will probably follow. On the downside the same patterns can be discerned. Let's say the bonds break hard and the S&Ps don't follow. On the next rally in bonds, the S&Ps will probably skyrocket higher.

Watching the S&Ps in relation to these other markets and indicators is the only way I know to read the market without actually being in the pit and watching the commercials, arbs, commission houses and locals interacting with one another.

Watch How One Market Behaves in Terms of Another

One more important clue: The real signal to watch for is when the indicators back off of a rally or react upward following a break. How does the stock market respond to a bond rally and reaction? Does it break hard or show signs of support? Conversely, how does the stock market behave in terms of a bond decline followed by a modest rally? Does it stay weak or snap back? Those are the real clues.

If the bonds were to break 20 points real fast, I'll guarantee that the S&Ps will go down as the locals sell on the bond break. The question is: *When the break reverses and the bonds rally a few points, what will the S&Ps do?* If they rally back strong, it means that the locals who were caught short had to pay up on the rally back. The commercials were *not* following them; in fact, they used the opportunity to become aggressive buyers. However, if the S&Ps continue to deteriorate while the bonds bounce off their break, you can make money by selling. The next time the bonds break the bottom is likely to fall out of the market.

At times, it helps to follow all four or five indicators to decide what you should do. My rule is to follow the trend when I'm thinking of loading up with a serious position. In a bear market I'll sell seriously into rallies; in a bull market, I'll buy aggressively on declines.

THE IMPLICATION OF HIGH VOLUME

Want a sure signal that a big move is coming—one that can make you some serious money? Look at the volume. In

August 1984 we were in a two-year-old bull market. Volume one day reached a phenomenal 100 million shares by noon. At that time, the record in S&Ps was about 130 million shares, so I knew we were having a big day. Because the Dow was already up 18 points at noon, the market was not likely to back off. Not with the high volume. I concluded that the market was going much higher. My strategy was to buy the market, then on its highs, and stand there with my hands in my pocket waiting for the market to run. I knew that if I sold and the market went higher, I'd have a hard time getting back in at a reasonable price.

The inclination is to sell on tiny breaks, but if you are serious about making money you can't bail out prematurely—especially in bull markets rising on high volume. That's where a lot of floor traders make their mistake. They are tempted to take a one- or two-tick profit because it is a sure thing. But who wants a tick in a market that is about to scream 500 higher?

Instead of looking for small profits, you should be asking: What's offered for sale? What's bid for to buy? Remember, if the market is going in one direction, getting out is going to be tricky, and getting back in even trickier. This is especially true if you trade big numbers. You can't scalp on large positions. Holding a position for three hours can be as emotionally draining as standing in a dark closet for two days, but you have to use discipline if you are going to make the big money.

Getting in, of course, is only half the story. You have to know when to get out. And that involves the most difficult question of all: How do you know when the rally is over? How can you tell when to get out? If the market really starts to run you can simply decide to sell "market on close" because the short sellers will be eager to buy on the close, and the market is likely to end the day substantially higher.

On that day in 1984, I kept buying all afternoon, thinking, "There's no way it can go past this point." But I was wrong. It can, and it did. If I've learned anything from the bull market, it is that when a market wants to run, it will. You can't stand in front of a freight train.

SPOOKING THE PIT

Some analysts say that the Dow could go to 5,000. If stocks are the only game in town, who says it can't? The problem with the S&P market is figuring out who's doing what—and why. For instance, big commercials engaged in program selling like to buy stocks and sell futures. They might be offering 200 or 300 cars every two or three ticks up. If you are standing in the S&P pit watching the action, you'll know what they are doing: Having sold 200 March S&Ps at a half, they will then buy IBM and other stocks. Nonetheless, it is frightening to see the heavy hitters doing so much selling. It misleads the locals into thinking that the S&P is declining.

That's what spooks the pit. The commercials don't have to come back and cover their sales because they've got the cash stocks. They don't care which way the market runs because they are making their money on the spread between cash and futures.

At times, the premium will encourage reckless buying and selling. The *premium* is the amount by which futures trades over cash; when futures trades under cash, it is known as a *discount*. We might have a 400-point premium right now, but when the premium gets down to, say, 200 points, the commercials will probably start buying. Before you know it, the premium will rise to 700 points. You can't just sell a premium market and buy a discount market. The entire issue is much more complex than that. A premium market reflects a bullish sentiment; the cash market may indeed spurt up and narrow the premium. Conversely, a discount market reflects a bearish sentiment.

WATCH FOR THE EXPLOSIVE BURST

I've often seen the S&Ps take hours to rally 80 points and then break 60 points in a minute—and vice versa. That kind of explosive burst is important because it indicates that the market has touched the highs of the day. On the slow breaks, the market will generally regain strength and move higher.

The general rule is: *Any fast move, from the bottom or the top, indicates the direction the market wants to take.* Of course, there are exceptions.

The speed of the move is critical. Fifty or 60 points in a minute is fast. I'm not talking about hitting the high and coming down a tick every five minutes or so. In that case, fresh buying is meeting the selling and pushing the market higher. That's why there's not much of a selloff. When you see that spike, it's time to position yourself for the move to come. A lot of traders miss the mark at this point because they don't understand what's happening.

Let's say you are long and the market is rallying up. Prices hit new highs and then suddenly—out of nowhere—the market collapses 70 points within seconds. That's a signal you don't want to miss. Yet traders tend to ask a bit much of the market, wanting it to rally back up before they sell it again. For example, if the high is even and the market then slides to 30, a lot of people might start sending in limit orders—sell 50 at 80, sell 50 at 75, and so on. The problem is, the market probably won't go back up there again for them to sell. It may rally briefly from 30 to a half or double, only to fail and power its way down below even. At that point, the people who are long will be forced out. They will lose 100 points off the high when they could have sold the market at a half or double. Once again, the quick burst is a sure clue that the market wants to run. You must jump quickly then or you will miss the move entirely.

In placing limit orders, it's not so important to sell near the high or buy near the bottom. The important thing is not to overstay the market. If you are wrong on the market, you need to correct yourself immediately—not after it is too late. Most customers miss getting out near the high of the day because they want one more shot at the top to get out. But they aren't going to get it. So don't try to put in a limit order near the high because it won't get hit. The market will start to slip, and you'll pay handsomely for your mistake.

THE SUREST SIGNAL

The rules for following the initial burst are simple: First, wait for the initial run to signal the direction; then, wait for a pullback; finally, load the boat and jump aboard. You want to let the market run a bit prior to taking your position so that you can see how far it goes.

While these rules may seem simple, in practice they are often difficult to follow. I can remember a day when the S&Ps were up about 40. I was trading fives and tens in the pit and nothing much was happening. Then I decided to buy 20 cars at 30, planning to sell them at 35. Instead, the market fell back to 20 then rallied back to 30. It was time to forget this position. So, on the next rally, I sold my contracts at 30, 35 and 40, barely breaking even on the trade. As soon as I exited the market, however, prices shot up to 55, where I immediately sold a couple of contracts. I saw no use in buying a market in the doldrums—the probabilities favored lower prices following a rally. But I was wrong. A moment later, the market rallied to the higher quarter. It seemed ironic that when I was loaded up with contracts, the market couldn't rally to save my life. Then, as soon as I got out, the market skyrocketed and I got killed. It was time to average my position, so I sold a couple more up at the top. I waited for a pullback to get me out even, but I had no such luck that day!

The market screamed higher. After I sold the final two cars at 30, it went 40, 50, 60, 70, 80, 90, even bid! Not even a down-tick! I was taking a loss on all four cars. Seeing my plight, the trader standing next to me said, "What are you waiting for? Can't you see it wants to go higher? Why aren't you bidding to get out of those short positions?"

He didn't understand that these four cars were meaningless to me. But he was definitely correct about the direction. Experiencing that sudden rally, I knew instinctively that on the next break it would be time to load the boat.

There was a little more left in the rally, then it started to break. It went quickly from 15 down to 80, hung around there a few seconds, and then went back up to even on one-lots. I told myself it wasn't time yet. The first minor break never shakes out the weak longs, but the next break would. On the second break, the people who were sitting on their profits would think that the move was over and would start selling—right when I began my heavy buying campaign.

MY BIG OPPORTUNITY

Watching the break begin, I stayed cool, giving no signals as to whether I was bullish or bearish. I could tell that most of the locals were long and eagerly awaiting higher prices. Keep in mind that the market had just rallied about 200 points in a couple of minutes. It only made sense that we would get at least a 50-point break. It's the move *after* the break that I was waiting for. But first I needed the break to put on my long positions near the bottom of the move.

As the market traded lower, the offers began—60, double, half—two, four, five contracts—that wasn't the kind of selling I was interested in. You can always get out small positions. I was looking for size. I was looking for someone to get a little careless and offer the wrong thing. It can happen, and it did.

A big local who stands near me in the pit suddenly offered, "Sell 50 at a half!"

"Buy 'em!" I screamed. I was on him in a second. He began to show signs of nervousness, realizing he had just made a big mistake. How was he going to get out of that 50-lot trade now? He'd been caught trying to shove the market lower to no avail. Actually, he was just trying to be a big shot and I'd called his bluff. Clearly, he was stuck.

Almost immediately, the market went higher from there. I started bidding on 50 cars at one-tick increments: 70 on 50; 75 on 50. I ended up buying all the 80 offers, about 60 cars in all. Then the people who had sold me the 70s and 80s started to get nervous.

As the Dow began to creep back up, the S&P flew up 100 points. After getting stuck on my four-lot trade, I was making it back in spades. The question now was: *Where do I get out?*

I decided to get out when the locals who had just sold me the 70s and 80s realized the party was over. Mob psychology would provoke a collective panic. They would make unrealistically high bids, and I would be there to sell them all they wanted. And that's precisely what happened.

CHAPTER TWENTY

The Pros and Cons of Doing Size

There are both advantages and disadvantages to being a large trader in the pit. Traders who deal in 50-lot orders are treated differently than those who do one-lots. Some brokerage houses recognize the difference and assign certain brokers to handle small one- to five-lot trades and others to execute larger orders. Brokers are also separated in terms of buying and selling. Thus, one broker in a large commission house might be in charge of executing the sell orders and another the buy orders. In general, brokers working for large houses are on salary. To them, it is just a job, albeit a high-pressure one.

Locals look to the brokers to generate the public "paper" they need to offset their large positions, especially when the locals find themselves on the wrong side of the market. To illustrate this point, let's say I'm short in the market and it begins to rally against me. I'm losing money and I need to get out. But because I'm a large trader, the pit will know that I want to buy size. That means they will probably bid the market up. My subsequent bidding will push it even higher, giving them an opportunity to sell at an inflated price. Consider my dilemma. I'll have to pay to get out. And because I need to buy a lot of contracts, I can't waste time with one- or two-lot orders. I'm looking for a broker who is executing a public order for 50 cars.

THE ADVANTAGE OF DOING SIZE

The customer doing size can often get very good fills, even selling the high or buying the bottom of the day, if he or she is willing to take the other side of a large local's trade. The need to trade size also explains why the locals usually stand in the same place in the pit everyday. A broker who wants to do size will look over to where one of the big locals stands. If I'm not in my spot, the broker will look elsewhere.

Let's say the market is trading at 70. A broker with a 50-lot order can get filled at 90 even though some 80s and 85s are available. Locals who are stuck in short positions will grab the offer. They know that if they hesitate, the market will soon rise to the upper quarter and they'll lose a lot of money. After all, the difference between a 90 fill and an upper quarter fill is $8,750 on 50 cars.

THE DISADVANTAGE OF DOING SIZE

One disadvantage of doing size is that the larger the trade, the more disruptive it is to the market. That's why prices fluctuate. A stable market can change instantly in response to new information. With a single bid we learn that Merrill Lynch wants to buy 200 contracts. If we had known that a moment ago, we would have sold at a higher price.

For a big trader, even a five- or ten-lot order can cause havoc in the pit. If all the locals are long and waiting for additional buying to push prices higher, a single ten-lot order from a paper-filler is enough to spook the pit. When the locals realize that they are all on the long side, they will panic and the market will free-fall once the selling starts.

YOUR OWN WORST ENEMY

Other locals who are trying to get out of the same positions are your competitors, but you can easily become your own worst enemy. For example, if you are short and the market is screaming higher, you'll have to bid up the market in order to find a willing seller to cover your position. But in doing so you are cutting your own throat. As soon as the pit knows you are in trouble, it will cost you another 50 points to get out. It's happened to me.

CHAPTER TWENTY-ONE _____

_____

Money Management

I know this is a paradox, but it is one that most customers need to understand: *On some of my best days, I don't make any money.*

The reason is this: On some of my best days, I lose a tremendous amount of money in the morning yet manage to get back near even by the close. There are days when I'll lose $50,000 before lunch, but by the close I may be down only $3,000. To me, that's a good day. Many new traders fail to realize the risk involved. To have the presence of mind to get the money back is a key ingredient to success. The winners will always take care of themselves. So if you can minimize the damage on losing days, you are well ahead of the game.

WHEN YOU ARE HOT

There's an entry in the prospectus offerings for one of my private funds in which I took just $3,569 during September 1984, and ran it up to $235,083 by month's end. That's a 6,586 percent increase. My style of trading is to push myself, to see how far I can take a relatively small amount of money. If I'm cold, I'll go back to the basics until I start to get good again. I'll put $20,000 in my account and pyramid like crazy to run the account to about $200,000 and start over again. That's what happened in September 1984.

SMALLER NUMBERS AFTER A HIT

As a money management tool, this seems to work for me: If I'm wrong and I take a $50,000 hit, I'll go back to trading twos and threes until I can build it back up. This may happen several times a year depending upon how active the markets are.

A lot of traders believe in taking time off after suffering a serious loss in the market. This doesn't work for me. After all, when you return, you're still facing those losses. What are you going to do in your free time, worry about your mistake? In any probability business like futures trading, you are going to have good days and bad days. If you want to be successful, you just have to say, "So what?" Then forget about it.

The day the space shuttle Challenger exploded I lost over $100,000. The next day I walked into the exchange as if nothing had happened. Why? Because I'm a professional. Would I have done anything differently? Sure, if I'd known what I know now. The world is made up of extenuating circumstances and there were plenty of them that day. These things happen, that's all.

Thinking about the money can get you in deep trouble. Take the public speculator who thinks, "I can't get out now—I've lost too much." That's the wrong attitude. It *can* get worse. Just think of January 8, 1986, or September 11 or 12 of that year—days when we had over 1,000-point ranges in the S&P. A lot of traders got buried in those sharp breaks. They thought they'd buy a little more until the next rally got them out of trouble. But the next rally never came.

WHEN YOU ARE COLD

Here's a surefire rule that you can't afford to ignore: *Don't try to get healthy in a hurry by increasing your financial commitment in the market.* It won't work. Pit professionals are well aware of the cycles of winning and losing, and they know who is hot and who is cold. Rumors about who is making money and who is getting killed fly through the air. So if I'm on a hot streak, no one in the pit will fade me on even a one-lot. But when I'm cold, they all want to be on my cards.

Not long ago, some of the pit traders were talking about a local who goes through very visible hot and cold spells. Everyone agreed that he was cold at that point. For weeks we watched him buy 40s and sell quarters, or buy halves and sell 35s. It was costing him about $5,000 to $10,000 a day.

On the day we were talking about him, he must have decided to stop being cold by doing big numbers. On the open, he bid double on 100. A very big trading house came in and shoved them right down his throat, selling him the whole 100 contracts.

He had no choice but to take them. He was getting mad. He was already long 10 cars from 45 and now he'd just bought 100 more at 55. He wanted the market to go higher, but he ended up selling them at 40 and 35.

You won't believe what happened next. The instant he sold his contracts, the market screamed higher. The buyers took the market up to even bid in no time. He lost control and started screaming at everyone in the pit. This could happen to anyone—the investor in Des Moines as well as the local on the floor. The point is, he never should have tried to get hot when he was cold.

SENDING FOOT SOLDIERS INTO THE PIT

The time to make a greater financial commitment in the market is when you have a clear indication that the market is in a mood to run. One way to find this out is to send in some orders. Professionals, who are primarily after information rather than good fills, send out small orders to see how they get treated. The information that's sent back by these "foot soldiers" can be invaluable. It's like General Patton sending out three or four soldiers as scouts during World War II. If the Germans replied by sending back 9,000 tanks, it would be overkill. But it would also tell Patton that it wasn't a good idea to invade that afternoon.

YOU ARE AFTER INFORMATION, NOT MONEY

I don't recommend the foot soldier approach for customers unless they understand the concept. Remember, you are not trying to make money with the orders; you are trying to gain valuable information. But, think about this: Say you purchase a single S&P futures at the market. You throw the order in and the market sinks out of sight. You are underwater almost immediately. Don't you think you'd want to get short in a meaningful way on the next rally? That's the kind of information I'm talking about. Trading this way on paper just isn't the same. You can't really judge the validity of the fills with paper trading. And, besides, your emotional commitment would be quite different.

HOW IT WORKS IN PRACTICE

Generally, I'm looking for an opportunity to put on my major position of the day during the early morning hours. If I think we are in for a big down day, I may start going short five to ten minutes after the open. Then, depending on the price action, I may add to the position, selling them higher or lower, for the next 30 to 40 minutes—ten contracts here, 20 contracts there, until I've acquired my desired size. Having acquired my position, of course, I have to ask: What if I'm wrong? If I am I'll have to pay up handsomely to get out of a big position. Understanding the risk, I know what to do if I'm wrong. But I'm not content to sit tight. I'll immediately start sending out soldiers on reconnaissance missions. I'm quite willing to sacrifice a few trades in order to see what's out there and, with good fortune, to get and keep the market moving in my direction.

Not long ago, for example, we had a selloff of more than 700 points from Friday's high to Monday's low. This immediately told me that we would have another selloff the following day. You don't get a big break like this without taking out the low the following day, according to the odds. Monday's price action told me to be a seller on Tuesday. The question was where?

Tuesday's open would provide the clue. Tuesday morning we got the bounce; it opened 70 points higher than Monday's close, a full 170 points higher than the previous low. Here was a real selling opportunity. At the open, I immediately sold the 70s. Then it rallied and I sold the 75s. Again, the market went higher, and I sold the 90s. It went all the way up to the higher 20. I was short from 70, 75 and 90 and the market was 220 points over Monday's low, yet I was still pretty certain we would go down to test the low.

Indeed, the market started to break, just hitting an airball. There were no bids. When a commerical offered 200 cars, the bottom fell out. The market went into a free-fall down to the lower 60 where a few bargain hunters bid on a few contracts.

As the market was breaking, I did my best to keep it moving down. So when the offer was 105, I offered one at even. Another local offered five at 95, so I offered one at 90. "At 85," a chorus of sellers yelled. "One at eighty!" I screamed.

A DANGEROUS GAME TO PLAY

Understandably, this is a dangerous game to play. I'm risking that a buyer will hit my offer and that I'll sell the low of the move. But I only offered one contract and, besides, the pit wasn't buying anything. I just helped it get where it really wanted to go a little faster. Actually, I was short from high above, so the risk was minimal. I don't mind losing on one contract to make profits on 20 or 30.

Needless to say, the big players, notably the commercials, didn't like this fast price action. So when they decided to join the fray, that determined the direction—in this case down. Whatever bullish enthusiasm existed prior to that point just disappeared. Finally, after the break took us down near Monday's low, I started covering the short positions. It stopped 40 points below Monday's low—right on target. Eventually, of course, it rallied and closed a little higher on the day. But what did I care? I'd already made my money on the real move of the day, the one the probabilities suggested.

I'm not recommending that public speculators try trading the market in this fashion. This is strictly a professional strategy. By sending in market orders, however, most customers occasionally accomplish the same thing inadvertently. But while they tend to sacrifice their main troops, I send in just a few expendable ones.

MAKE CAREFUL PREDICTIONS

Without trying to sound immodest, I have something that very few people have—the ability to walk into the exchange and make money almost every day.

Whether it is one dollar or a hundred thousand dollars, you have to concentrate on that same goal of making money. You have to play the game. Can you make big money every day? I don't think so. And I don't think you should try. On the other hand, when you have a shot at making some serious money, go for it. But to consistently try to predict the big days is to ask for trouble. Approaching the market as if you are stepping up to the plate to hit the long ball is a big mistake. The market may not be in the mood for the long ball—and if it isn't, you lose. When I make the wrong play, I can lose up to $50,000. Unfortunately, these big trading hits are part of the game.

DON'T BE AN EDGE TRADER

Edge traders are normally found in the trading pits, but many public customers try this difficult feat from off the floor. Essentially, the edge trader tries to buy at the bid and to sell the market at the offer. The difference between the bid and the ask constitutes the "edge." The probelem with this strategy, which is essentially scalping, is that it often leaves bearish investors long the market, and, conversely, bullish investors short.

Edge trading is a risky short-term strategy because volatile markets will kill you when you are wrong. Yet it is inviting because it seems like sure money. Unfortunately, the profits are anything but sure. In fact you often have to risk thousands to gain hundreds—a poor risk/reward ratio in anyone's book.

In my early days, I traded Treasury bond futures before the S&P market opened in 1982. It was a time when bonds were down in the 60s and 50s. I was real bearish on bonds, but in the pit, the edge traders were looking for their tick or two.

The edge is an elusive concept today because it can evaporate in a second. The scalper mentality of edge traders keeps them from seeing the real risk they take in gaining the edge on a trade. If the market is at 90, grabbing the edge by buying the 80s won't be very good if the market breaks to 30. But this is precisely what happens repeatedly in the S&Ps. On a break like that, the bargain hunters will rush in, only to be crushed a minute later. What good is the edge in such a situation?

I remember a day in the bond market when the market was trading at 14 and the edge traders were, naturally, trying to buy a tick lower at 13. Wanting to be short in a serious way, I hit all the bids. I went around the pit and sold them all they wanted. They thought they were getting an incredible deal. Most floor traders consider it bad etiquette to give up the edge, but the locals thought of it as free money, planning, of course, to sell them at 14 for a one-tick profit. That's also why the pit loves when customers send in market orders. The brokers usually give the edge to the locals. So you can imagine their delight when I gave them the edge and the market rose a point to 15 on their 14 bid. I must have sold at least 70 cars. I was happy. They were happy. I got short in a big way, and they got the edge. It was an edge trader's dream—until the bottom fell out. The market suddenly dropped about 1-8/32nds, or about 40 points. A lot of good those one-tick edges did.

Pretty soon, with panic in their eyes, they were all demanding bids from me. But I didn't budge because the market was going down. Just for the hell of it, when the bids had dried up completely, I bid on a couple way below the last posted price. By then, of course, the market was free-falling. So my bid was it.

Naturally, it wasn't long before they came in as sellers at the low of the day. When something like that happens, a basic law of the market prevails: *When a trader holds onto a losing position in a deteriorating market and finally decides to get rid of it, that's the bottom or the top. From there, the market will be free to go the other way*. And that's exactly what happened. The market soon rallied.

Once the edge traders had butchered themselves by selling at the bottom, I began a buying campaign. I helped bid it up from there. These edge traders thought they were getting a tremendous deal buying 13s in a 14-bid market. The point is: *If it is terrible, sell it; if it is good, buy it. Don't think about the edge.* It will only get you in trouble.

A Few Good Rules

Much of the volatility in the S&P market is created by the locals, who often find themselves on the wrong side of the market at the same time. When the whole pit decides to sell at once, the bottom falls out. The locals will sell at any price to attract buyers, even if it means offering down.

Many of the locals on the floor are young—the average age in the S&P pit is probably about 30—and few of them have any serious money. Aside from the big locals and the veterans—those who consistently make money— the locals are probably the most undercapitalized of all the players. If they don't get out quickly when the market moves against them, they may not be able to come back and trade tomorrow.

20-LOT TRADES ON $10,000 MARGIN

If a small-time local buys 20 cars at 60 and pretty soon it is double offer, he or she is going to be selling halves and 40s. This little trader and about 40 other locals who find themselves in the same situation are going to panic and drive the market lower. That's what causes big price swings—fear and greed. The local who buys a 20-lot with only $10,000 in a margin account is going to get killed. At a loss of $500 a tick, a ten-second, 50-point drop can do a lot of damage. You can bet he's going to be selling. That can create the opportunity you are looking for.

RULE #1: THE MOVE WILL BE FALSE IF ONLY THE LOCALS ARE INVOLVED

You can make money on these moves if you keep things in perspective. In the S&P, it is difficult to distinguish a real move from a fakeout. Remember, *the move will be false if only the locals are involved.*

RULE #2: SELL AFTER SHARP BREAKS AND BUY AFTER SHARP RALLIES

Off the trading floor, it can be hard to tell whether a move is legitimate or not. How do you know whether the locals have engineered the move or whether the arbs and commercials are in there in a big way? As a general rule, *if the market is rallying and suddenly breaks 50 or 60 points in a few seconds, sell on the next rally.* If it breaks only 20 or 30, the rally will proceed and the market will head higher. The reverse is true on the downside: *If the market is breaking and then rallies 70 or 80 points, buy it on the next break.*

RULE #3: THE MOVE AT THE TOP AND BOTTOM WILL BE FAST

These guidelines are also useful in knowing when to exit the market if you are already long or short. How do you know it is the bottom when the market is breaking? Or the top when it is rallying? The best indicator is speed. Look for the fast rally to run through the high and take two or three powerful, fast shots at the new highs. This will be the final high, and then it will break. Often, the break will be as fast as the rally because the locals have all been caught. That's where speed comes in. For example, if the market touches even on the run up and is at 45 moments later, you have to get out on the next rally to 75. In getting out, remember that the market will trade at the high tick for only a second or two. Forget about limit orders. Sell at the market. Go retail and get out.

MIT ORDERS AS AN ALTERNATIVE

Here's where you might have a problem with limit orders. Many traders don't realize that *if the market trades at your limit price, there is no guarantee that you are filled.* Some brokers are better at getting orders off than others, so you may or may not be filled. In the free-for-all atmosphere of the pit, there's also no guarantee that the fill will get back to you promptly. So there you are left in the dark while the market jumps around. What do you do? One strategy is to use a *market-if-touched (MIT)* order. If the price on that order is touched, you will get filled somewhere.

FAST MARKETS

You want to be careful about a fast market when you throw in a market order. Remember that in a fast market, the boards lag far behind the trading prices in the pit. Let's say you have an order in to sell 5 cars at 80 MIT. When you put in the order, the market might be at 20. Before you know it, a rally begins: 30, 40, 50, 60, 70, 80, 90. Then the other way: 70, 60, 50, right down to 20 again. With a market-if-touched order, you know you are out. But if you decide to throw in a market order when you see 90 on the screen, here's what will happen: Your broker will call in the order. When it reaches the floor, it will be given to a runner or hand-signaled into the pit. By the time the runner gets to the S&P pit, you might get filled at 35. That's the problem with market orders.

Contrary Opinion Trading—How To Bet Against the Crowd

Very few people can win in the futures market, so betting against the crowd shouldn't come as a novel idea, especially at major tops and bottoms in the market. One guideline I look for is a headline in a major publication such as the *Chicago Tribune* or *The Wall Street Journal*. You can be sure that once the information is front-paged across America the end is near. So what's an inkling that the bull market is over? "STOCKS SOAR. BIGGEST VOLUME IN HISTORY. NO END IN SIGHT." When you read that, you'll know the end is near.

A CONTRARIAN COFFEE COUP

In my office one morning, my trading assistant announced that her mother heard news of an impending coffee shortage. In fact, her mother was so impressed with this news that she immediately purchased 25 cans of coffee at $1.70 a can. When I heard the story I thought, "I don't trade coffee much, but this is a sure sign that we are at a top."

I raced to the floor and immediately put in an order to

sell short coffee futures in New York. Three days later, I was ahead by $4,000 on each contract. I bought in my short positions and thanked my trading assistant for the information. Do you know of an easier way to figure the market?

WHEN THE CROWD WANTS TO SELL GOLD—BUY!

This contrarian approach can be very accurate. I had friends who purchased gold stocks for pennies years ago. By 1980, when gold had risen to $850 an ounce, the stocks were worth plenty. These people were sure that the penny stocks, which had already risen to more than $20 a share, were about to explode to $100 a share. But where are they now? They are penny stocks again. And those hapless investors are still holding the stocks. I've told them to let me know when they decide to sell their gold stocks because I *know* that will be the bottom. That's how the markets work.

"GRAIN MARKETS—NO BOTTOM"

A perfect example of this phenomenon occurred in the grain markets in 1980. That was the year soybeans went down from about $9.00 to $6.50 per bushel in ten trading days. And when was it over? On the Friday the *Chicago Tribune* headlined: "GRAIN MARKETS—NO BOTTOM." The following day, soybeans opened limit-down and closed limit-up. The top in a bull market will occur the same way, but in reverse: On the day the bull market ends, the market will open a lot higher and close a lot lower. That will be the sign that it is finally over.

HUMAN PSYCHOLOGY

Don't underestimate human psychology in these markets. People are people, regardless of whether they have money or not, so logic doesn't always work. If you want a sure sign of when a bull or bear market is over, you have to wait until the market drives out everybody the wrong way. So if you are looking for a bull market top, be assured the market will skyrocket first. This will serve to drive out every short seller who ever dreamed of selling the market. Tremendous short covering will drive the market much higher than anyone ever dreamed. Only then will the market decline. This is the classic signal. And at the bottom the reverse will be true. Premature buyers who attempt to pick a bottom will be driven out good and hard so that the lesson will last. Once the damage has been done, the market will, of course, be free to rise.

You have to be careful on days when the market is forming a major top or bottom. If you participate on the wrong side of the market on those days, you will regret it. There will be record volume, and the moves will be severed.

MARKETS ARE IRRATIONAL

Whenever you get the urge to understand why the market behaves as it does, remember that markets are driven by human behavior, which is generally irrational. That's why econometric and computer models are so far off base. They attempt to generate scientific numbers from irrational behavior.

Let me give you an example of this irrational behavior. Several years ago, the hard money gurus were telling their subscribers to buy copper futures at 85¢ per pound because, they reasoned, the cost of production was at least $1 a pound. Because it is uneconomical to sell a product below the cost of production, copper seemed to be a sure bet. The problem was that while on the surface this argument perhaps seemed logical, the facts of the matter were different. If you are a third-world dictator heading up a corrupt regime and copper is your only export, when prices fall you simply produce twice as much. These dictators don't care what some economist from the Chase Manhattan Bank thinks. They are going to produce more copper. And that's exactly what happened. As a result, the price of copper plummeted to levels from which it has yet to recover. The investors, of course, lost their money.

THREE GOOD ASSUMPTIONS

Because markets are irrational, you have to formulate assumptions that take this irrationality into account. Remember, market forecasting is an art, not a science. Three good assumptions to follow are:

1. There are other forces besides profit and loss that fuel markets. Fear and greed are two examples.
2. There are many extenuating circumstances that have nothing to do with the numbers that play themselves out in the market.
3. Markets do not act rationally.

NO REASONED ANSWER

Unless you understand and accept these concepts, I don't care how many charts you pore over or how many technical or fundamental indicators you follow, you aren't going to make it in the market. Markets are irrational. There simply isn't a "reasoned" answer to everything that happens, the nightly television reports to the contrary. Take the typical technical analyst, for example. Technicians maintain that everything is reflected in price behavior. They look at a chart, see a head and shoulders pattern, and all of a sudden a big news event comes along and the price breaks through the support or resistance. Would the prices have broken without the news event? Perhaps. On the surface, the technical approach may make sense, but is it enough?

Sometimes the big players can't enter the game without tipping their hands. Think about Bunker Hunt in the silver fiasco. Imagine what would have happened if he'd started selling silver before they changed the rules against him.

Word would have gotten out and the prices would have collapsed on him anyway. Even if he had turned bearish, his size would have driven the market lower. There is nothing he could have done about it. Did the charts signal a top? Perhaps they did, but let's face it: The markets operate on psychology. They don't call them futures markets for nothing.

When the bull market in stocks began in August 1982, there was no bullish consensus on Wall Street until the Dow was well past 1,100. Why? Because there was no evidence to indicate a bull market was about to get under way. Right now, the situation is the same in the gold market. No one wants to advocate owning gold because inflation is not a factor. The handwriting isn't on the wall just yet. A portfolio manager with an enormous inventory of bonds is unlikely to talk about a pickup in inflation because, with that inventory, what else could he or she say?

The markets will tell you in advance when something is brewing. Right now, the gold and platinum markets are showing signs of moving much higher. The analysts blame the turmoil in South Africa. South Africa has been in turmoil for ten years, and Iran and Iraq have been at war for more than seven years. Have these events affected the price of gold? No. But television news reports blame South Africa for the latest rise in gold prices—as if something new were happening in the region. The only thing that fuels gold prices is inflation. Think about it. We've had good news for three years now: Oil prices were cut from $30 to $10 a barrel; interest rates plummeted; gold prices dropped. The next move is bound to be much higher.

When gold prices get to $1,500, I want to ask all the pundits where they were when it was trading at $350 an ounce. *I* don't want to buy gold at $1,500 an ounce. At that price, I'm going to sell the gold I bought at the bottom. Analysts act like this because they have no feel for the market. They think in terms of numbers.

This overemphasis on numbers gets especially confusing when you think about the highly publicized indexes such as the government's consumer price index. In the past ten years they have changed the way these numbers are calculated over and over again. They have doctored the numbers to suit their purposes just as Dow Jones changes its industrial average when a company goes bankrupt. When International Harvester went bankrupt, it was removed from the Dow. When Johns Manville went bankrupt, the same thing happened. Companies like that are bad for business. So when you try to interpret statistics, whether the government kind or stock index averages, you have to remember that the authorities can change the rules any time it suits their purposes.

DON'T USE CHARTS AS A CRUTCH

An overemphasis on price charts is another sign of following the crowd. Pit traders as a group are fond of charting the price action on point-and-figure charts. Indeed, Chicago printing shops have discovered that selling the pre-printed grids to floor traders has become a minor cottage industry. Most traders in the S&P rely on a 5 X 20 or 10 X 30 reversal. But do charts help? I don't think so. If anything, they provide an artificial crutch, something to blame if a trade doesn't work out. At a seminar I gave in Cleveland last year, a member of the audience asked my opinion of charts. My reply: *I suspect there is an inverse relationship between the amount of time and study that goes into charts and the amount of money one ultimately extracts from the market.*

He laughed, but he knew I was serious. Sure I rely on charts, but only the ones I keep in my head. The traders who make money keep the charts in their heads. You really don't have time to fool around with plotting X's and O's on tiny grids, trying to figure the breakout points. Besides, that's what concentration is all about. When a market breaks and it stops, I remember *where* it stopped.

When it rallies back, I remember *where* it stopped rallying. I remember where the big orders are. I keep this kind of information in my head, so I don't need a chart in my hand.

THE PERFECT SCENARIO

Sometimes overwhelming one-sidedness in the market suggests just that—strength or weakness. Moves such as these should *never* be faded. When attempting to decide on a contrarian or noncontrarian approach, the impact of volatility on the market cannot be underestimated. When the market runs—either up or down—it makes the pit extremely bullish or bearish. This, of course, will have an impact on prices. As a rule, therefore, you can view a big move in the market as a sign of potential *additional* strength or weakness to follow. Typically, if the Dow Jones industrial averages rise or fall more than 20 or 25 points, the following day will usually see a similar move in the same direction. That's because the bullish or bearish enthusiasm rarely dissipates in less than 48 hours. The price action on September 12, 1986, the day following the 86-point break in the Dow Jones industrials, comes to mind as an example of this phenomenon.

Let's consider a hypothetical example. Assume the Dow closes up 30 and the next morning the bonds are trading slightly lower. The lower bond market will cause some weak longs to have second thoughts, so the S&Ps might open mixed and trade down 15 or 20 points. That's the immediate selloff I'm looking for. On a lower opening and a slight selloff just moments after the open following a big day in the stock market, I'm going to buy everything in sight. Why? Because the probabilities are just not there for the Dow to go up 30 one day and down 17 the next.

In such a situation, you can almost buy with impunity because you know that at some time during the day the previous day's high is going to be met or taken out. The reverse is true on the downside.

Let me give you an example. Several Mondays ago, the Dow was down approximately 45 points. I made money on Tuesday by selling every rally in the pit. We went down to the lows on Tuesday *about nine times.* The bearishness was so prevalent in the pit that day that when the Dow rallied, nothing happened. But every time the Dow backed off a point, there was panic. In an up market, the reverse is true: *You want to buy the breaks on the following day.*

To illustrate this point, let's compare Friday, June 13, 1986, a big up day in the September S&P contract, with the following trading day, Monday, June 16, 1986. The prices for the two days are as follows:

September S&P 500

Friday, June 13, 1986	Monday, June 16, 1986
Open = 244.20	Open = 248.65
High = 248.70	High = 249.10
Low = 244.20	Low = 247.50
Close = 248.15	Close = 248.60

On June 13, 1986, the September contract opened on the low and closed almost 400 points higher. That was the key to the following day's price action. Thus, on Monday, you had to buy those breaks in anticipation of Friday's high (248.70) being reached or violated to the upside. Sure enough, we got that pop and prices rose up through the previous high and closed just two ticks off the previous high. This illustrates what I mean about the market tipping its hand. Strength is followed by strength and weakness by weakness. The previous high is a key resistance area that should be targeted as a selling area for the previously acquired long positions.

THE 20-POINT RULE

There is one simple rule that will earn you good profits if you follow it and trade the signals. First, watch how the Dow closes on any given trading day and on the following day take a position based on the Dow's direction. Specifically, the rule says:

• *If the Dow closes 20 or more points higher on the day, look to buy immediately on any lower open the following day.*

• *If the Dow closes 20 or more points lower on the day, look to sell immediately on any higher open the following day.*

If you take this initial position and the market moves against you, double up by taking *twice as many* positions as the original at .75 points under the opening price. (If you are a seller, of course, take twice as many positions as the original at .75 points higher than the opening price.) If the market can't stabilize and move in a favorable direction by the time you double up, chances are it is the wrong position. Hence, place a stop 1.30 points under the open if you are buying or a stop 1.30 points higher than the open if you are selling.

Where to take profits? A good area for the market to meet resistance is just above the previous day's high—about .30 to .50 points higher. So if you are a buyer on a day following a big rally on the Dow, look for the previous day's high to be violated by approximately .30 to .50 points. If you are a seller, the support will be just below the previous day's low—again, about .30 to .50 points.

TRADING FAST MARKETS

When a market wants to get somewhere in a hurry, it is a sign that there is a lot of one-sided pressure on prices. As a result, it is best to wait for the market to tip its hand and then follow by placing an order on the side of the initial spurt in prices. The speed with which the move is made is critical. A 100-point move in ten minutes is more significant than a 100-point move in two hours. For this reason, in trading fast markets, look for a 100-point move in less than 15 minutes. The direction of the move will signify the side of the market that you'll want to trade. If it goes 100 up, you'll be a buyer; if it goes 100 down, a seller. Once you know what to look for in terms of direction and time, you'll need a rule for placing the order. What should you look for? When buying, place your order at the first 30 percent break. If you get a 50 percent retracement, double up by buying twice as many contracts. If the market can't hold at the 50 percent retracement level, chances are you are wrong. In that case, place the stop at two-thirds, or 66 percent, of the initial rally from low to high. The same rules apply in reverse for declining markets. A sharp down move within the 15-minute time frame calls for selling short on the first 30 percent retracement. This order is followed by selling twice as many contracts on a 50 percent retracement. Again, if the rally persists, chances are the market is indeed headed higher. So place the stop to buy back the contracts at the two-thirds, or 66 percent, retracement level.

CHAPTER TWENTY-FOUR

January 1987—
The Customers Get Even

January 1987 was a classic example of the way a bull market works—a time when all the rules by which floor traders swear didn't work, when all that was required to win big was to buy the market and hold on. There was only one rule for winning in January 1987—buy! Where you bought didn't matter. You could have bought every rally and made money. You could have bought every Friday and sold every Wednesday. You could have bought anywhere and made money. It was a market tailor-made for customers who wanted to enrich themselves at the expense of the floor. It was, in every sense, a time when the customers got even.

THE FLOOR CAUGHT UNAWARE

A little background on the January rally. The Christmas holidays are a time when traders, especially the big traders, put the market out of their minds and try to enjoy the good life for which they've worked so hard all year. So in mid-December traders scatter around the world—to Australia, to Europe, to skiing resorts in the Rockies—to get away from the pressure-filled pits of Chicago. They take time out to tally up winnings, to put aside cash for taxes and to party. It was against this festive holiday atmosphere that the January rally caught a number of floor traders off-guard. They began the new year on a discordant note as the Dow opened $35 higher on the day and, within minutes, the S&P market gained 1,000 points without a retracement in price. The floor trader's approach to rallies is to sell. The customer's approach is to buy. So you can bet there was a lot of wonderment about this new market in the opening session of 1987.

It soon became apparent that we were looking at a real rally—a real bull market that was gathering strength even as the short coverers began bidding into the offers. That's when I realized there was nothing for sale anywhere. There were just buyers. So the short sellers, now chastened for their reckless selling, found themselves in a bidding war with one another as they reached to get their bids met. It was the classic bull market pattern.

Several months before the January rally I filmed a video titled "Confessions of a Floor Trader," in which I explained how to trade a bull market. "In a bull market," I'd stressed, "when the market opens steady to lower, it is just driving out the weak longs. As the day progresses, the market will get stronger, so you have to buy every open in a bull market that is steady to lower." Now, ten months later, this precise pattern was occurring day after day!

Sometimes on the floor you get the feeling that the stock market is so deep that, aside from occasional debacles like the 86-point drop in the Dow that day in September, you can't have the incredible swings we've been having recently. But, with the new tax laws and other factors operating in today's economy, the stock market is beginning to act like a high-flying, leveraged commodity future. During the January rally, you could have bought S&P futures anywhere and made big money. You could have bought them at the top of every rally and still made money. You could have been killed on the fill and still made money. So that three- or four-week period in January 1987 was significant in the sense that, for the first time, the customers got even.

There is a public perception that the people on the floor are the ones who make most of the money. The floor traders can take advantage of market orders, they have resources available to them, they have lower margin requirements and access to the pit—advantages that make the public speculator feel that he or she is operating at a severe disadvantage. What was significant about January 1987 was that all these perceived advantages didn't make any difference.

In January 1987, the retail people kept buying the S&Ps and making money everyday. Who do you think was selling to them? The floor. So for a whole month, the floor lost money while public customers made money. This was one time when it was better to be a customer in Des Moines buying S&Ps and holding on than a hotshot pit trader trying to pick tops and bottoms. The pit traders' attempts to scalp the market during January were an exercise in futility. Everybody was selling because it had always sold off before. But this time it was different.

THE OLD RULES

Consider some of the old rules that the pit has sworn by for years: Watch IBM, watch the bond market. During the first part of January, IBM fell from 128 to 115. The bonds, after trading at 102, dropped a couple of points. Taking these old signals as their clues, the locals were selling. The customers, meanwhile, were buying. And the market kept rising. This made the locals think that if they could just get it lower on the day, a ton of sell orders would hit the pit. The problem was they never got it lower. At 1:30 P.M., after being up all morning, the market climbed even higher.

Fueled by panic, everyone who was short decided to get out, and the next thing you know, we had a serious rally on our hands. We had 200-, 300-, 400- and even 500-point afternoon rallies every afternoon during January. It happened like clockwork day after day.

THE AFTERMATH

It is still too soon to tell, but I suspect that the aftermath of this big rally will be the customers giving the money back to the locals. It doesn't have to happen, but I suspect it will. Many customers don't realize that they walked into an extraordinary circumstance—one in which their good fortune is not likely to continue. In the aftermath of an incredible victory, most customers probably feel pretty good about their market judgment. The smart thing to do, of course, is to walk away with the money. But most customers will not do that.

We've already seen a day in which the Dow dropped an unprecedented 120 points in ten minutes. That's when the locals got some of their losses back fast. I'd heard rumors that there was a 7,000-lot order to sell at the market top. I didn't see it, but when we got to the top, the market collapsed. In the process of filling that single order, the market broke 500 points. After that, it rallied back about 250 points and then went straight down 1,400 points. That's when all the customers who had been long for weeks got killed. They had been sitting on paper profits for weeks, and out of nowhere the market collapsed like a rock. There were stops that day that got filled 1,000 points lower. How's that for slippage? You want to sell at 276 on a stop order and you get filled at 266. That's a $5,000 loss on a single contract!

I suspect that we'll have more volatile runs in the S&Ps similar to the ones we have just seen. The customers have to realize that a bull market cannot continue forever.

Here's a rule you want to make a note of: You want the trends and the corrections to occur at specific times during the day. Generally speaking, 11:00 A.M. until 1:30 P.M. central time is when the corrections occur. Thus, if the market opens higher and is strong in the early morning, it will generally spend the time from 11:00 A.M. to 1:30 P.M. correcting. Then, if there is anything left, it will resume after 1:30 P.M. With the big rally out of the way early, the market often lacks the follow-through to gain additional ground. This is the kind of clue that will prove to be very helpful.

WHEN TO BE CAREFUL

How do you tell when the big break will occur? By the action on the open. When it opens and immediately screams 300 or 400 higher, watch out! That's the day to be careful.

Many of my clients wanted to go long during the January runup, but I was taking a cautious approach. I heard stories from brokers who had clients who were long a couple hundred cars from 2,000 points lower. They made fortunes, but they gave up 1,000 points on the day when the market broke like a house of cards. There's no excuse for sitting on paper profits of that magnitude. The correction was long overdue.

The point is, customers can continue to get even with the floor by trading intelligently. A customer who had followed the advice in my video during January could have retired on that three-week move. And they could have spotted the top by the price action. If customers learn that the market can reverse in a hurry at key tops, they can continue to get even.

PART 4

What's Ahead

CHAPTER TWENTY-FIVE ─────────

Program Trading

The market has changed considerably since stock index futures were introduced. At first, the big financial institutions—banks, mutual funds, pension funds and brokerage houses—took a wait-and-see attitude toward the new markets. But in the last couple of years, the institutions have come to dominate trading. Perhaps the most significant new market strategy, which has enjoyed some play in the press, is program trading.

Program trading involves buying or selling a "basket" of stocks that roughly corresponds to the leading stocks in the S&P index and buying or selling an offsetting amount of stock index futures. The difference between gains or losses in the stock market and gains or losses in the stock index futures market constitutes profit. As long as the gain on one leg of the transaction offsets the loss on the other, the trade will return a profit.

Program trading is usually instituted in high premium markets and high discount markets. A *premium market* is one in which the futures price exceeds the cash price of the underlying index; a *discount market* is one in which the futures price is lower than the cash price. At any given time, the market may be trading at a premium or a discount, depending on market conditions. The thinking behind program trading is that the futures will inevitably come into line with cash prices. In fact, at the expiration of the futures contracts—there are four each year on the third Friday of March, June, September and December—the futures price *becomes* the cash index price. Thus, the program trader can capture the premium by selling futures and the discount by buying futures. That's the theory. In practice, of course, there can be a number of intervening factors. What happens, for instance, if the cash stocks don't move with a high degree of correlation with the index?

Program trading attracts a lot of publicity for the price swings it creates on quarterly expiration dates, known on the Street as the "triple witching hour." This is when stock options, options on futures and stock index futures all expire. Program trading strategies are relatively complicated, involving futures, options and securities, and the only given of the triple witching hour is that program traders will be "evening up," or offsetting previously acquired positions. The gyrations are created by the cross-currents of buying an instrument in one market and selling another in a related market. And because most of the trading takes place in the final moments of trading, the enormous volume can cause the market to skyrocket or plummet. That's what happened on Friday, March 21, 1986. As the triple witching hour approached, all appeared normal at the New York Stock Exchange. The Dow was down only eight points at 3:30 P.M. eastern time, just 30 minutes prior to the close. It later closed 36 points down on the day, the fourth biggest break in history at the time. The sharp decline, of course, precipitated a similar break in the S&P market in Chicago. Enormous profits and losses were generated in those final moments.

How can small traders, without millions of dollars at their disposal, cope with program trading? Well, for one,

I'd guard against the impulse to make simplistic trading decisions based on the day-to-day price spreads between futures and cash. Premium markets often become higher premium markets, and the same can be said of discount markets. After all, futures command a premium to the cash market because the overall market sentiment is bullish. Who's to say it won't become more bullish tomorrow? So selling into a premium market isn't the way to cash in on program trading. You have to remember that because of their cash ties, the commercials and other leading program traders don't care about the overall direction of the market—only the spread. They can sell enormous amounts of stock index futures contracts in a bull market and not lose money because they own the underlying stocks.

In general, program trading tends to magnify price moves. The bullish days become more bullish, and the bearish days become more bearish. This can be beneficial to the trader who knows how they operate and how to predict their behavior. Program trading decisions are made primarily by computer analysis of the market. And program players, like other big traders, tend to follow the trend. So on a day when the Dow is up, say, 18 points in the morning, the buy programs might very well push it another ten or 15 points in the afternoon. Whenever the market gets one-sided, the smaller players have very little choice but to go along. So as the closing bell approaches and the cash index is sitting on its high, without a flurry of selling the market can only go up as the short sellers run for the exits. If you are a speculator in stock index futures, you might want to stick around for the closing minutes on days when you are on the right side of the market and exit early when you sense you are wrong.

PERFORMANCE-MINDED MANAGERS ENSURE INCREASED VOLATILITY

In the future, program trading is likely to have even a greater impact on the market. The enormous volume surge that has occurred in the stock market over the last several years is directly attributable to the development of sophisticated new strategies using index futures and options. The new orientation toward short-term trading strategies as opposed to investment strategies has made today's money manager increasingly performance-minded. To gain that performance, money managers are going to use all available tools including program trading with options and futures.

Despite the controversy involving program trading and the "triple witching hour," industry leaders have shown little interest in changing the system. Not long ago, a group of investment houses, stock exchange officials and federal regulators met to try and resolve precisely why the expiration day volatility has exploded and how it could be moderated. They found that the price swings were more a public relations issue than a genuine market phenomenon. They concluded that index options and futures have added to the liquidity of the markets. So program trading and the violent swings associated with it are likely to persist. For speculators like me, who know how to read the market, greater volatility means more opportunity.

Yet, for those who haven't recognized the change in the market brought about by program trading, the new rules can be disconcerting. In the S&P pit we've seen hedgers and program traders sell as many as 15,000 contracts in a couple of days and then come back into the market a week later and lift the position. Do you know what that does to the market? First it pushes the market on the downside; then it pushes the market more by supporting it on the upside. The market would be breaking, the Dow would be falling and the commercials would suddenly come in bidding ten on a couple of hundred, 20 on a couple of hundred, 40 on a couple of hundred. Bids like these were killing the locals. Then, after the market absorbed those orders and traded lower again, the commercials would come back in and bid it up. The locals were getting hurt because they hadn't adapted to the new rules. When you're standing in the middle of the pit and experiencing this price action, you can't always see what's behind it. It has taken me time to figure out the new rules, but many traders haven't even recognized that the game has changed.

CHAPTER TWENTY-SIX _____

Rewriting the Rule Book

The traditional rules don't work anymore. Essentially, you can take the last 60 years of proven strategies and throw them away. They don't mean anything anymore. The market is jittery, and the brokers in the pit seem frightened. I don't know what it is. They get an order for ten contracts and treat it like a hot potato. They are afraid to hold onto anything. Several fights have broken out in the pit recently. If there's a 15 bid and somebody does a trade at a quarter, a fight will break out.

"Hey, I'm offering 15," a local will say. "What the hell are you doing?"

And the broker will say, "Well, I didn't hear you. That's why I'm bidding quarters."

Pretty soon, they'll be shoving each other over the misunderstanding. And then the security guards will haul them out of the pit. That's when the fists start flying and threats are made about writing people up and taking them upstairs before the pit committee. The point is, all this uneasiness is telling us something: *When the bull market ends, it is going to be disastrous. And if you don't do your* homework, and don't follow the advice outlined in this book, you are likely to get wiped out.

RECENT PATTERNS

You only have to consider some of the recent patterns to see how the market has changed in the past few months. The market has been hitting new highs by two or three ticks, then dropping 50, then rallying sharply. It is very difficult for a local—let alone a customer—to trade that pattern. Let's say a broker offers 200 contracts. A local reasons that no one will take out the order, and that will put an end to the move. So he or she has a resistance to sell against. But, lately, that reasoning has been wrong. Nowadays the order is absorbed. As soon as the broker offers 200 cars, someone buys them. Local ABC might buy 100, local XYZ might buy 50 and a third local might take the other 50. So much for the resistance. Now you have a whole new ball game.

There was a time when a few commercials could stop a rally simply by offering at the top. After all, who would want to fade that kind of financial muscle? But not today. The locals and the commercials can try to finesse it to go their way, but they are limited in their influence. They can make it get there a hair faster or slow it down a bit, but that's all. One of two things will happen if you try to muscle the S&P today. Either you are going to make it get there a little more quickly if you are right or you are going to get it shoved down your throat if you are wrong.

AN EX-MEMBER TRIES TO
MUSCLE THE S&P MARKET

The public thinks the market can be manipulated. We might get away with certain shenanigans in the commodities markets, but it doesn't work in the S&P. More than a few people have gotten blown out of the water trying to muscle that market.

I can remember an incident that occurred several months ago to a broker I'll call John who made an excellent living as a trader and order filler at the Merc for years. John filled paper for the major retail and commercial houses, in addition to trading for his own account. He wasn't some novice 30-year-old who leased a seat for $900 a month and decided to take his chances in the S&P pit.

Several months ago we were having one of those wild days when the market was all over the board. It would break a couple of hundred points, regain some strength, rally and take out the highs, and then collapse again. The locals in the pit were totally confused. I noticed that John sold ten or 15 cars at a half and 60. I thought this might be significant because as both order filler and local, a broker like John can influence many locals in the pit. Order fillers will often sell a few cars for their own account when they sense a resistance area. That's because they might have a bunch of orders to sell but none to buy. That is a clue that some orders are overhanging the market. If, for instance, there are a lot of sell orders at 20 or 25, the brokers can sell the 10s and 15s, thinking the top is just a little bit higher.

Big orders have the effect of spooking the pit. Accordingly, if a major player wants to sell size, you usually don't want to fade that trade. Why? Simply because big players have cash connections and excellent information—indeed, in the case of the big commercials, they *are* the stock market. So you can understand why the locals get spooked when one of the big players steps up to the plate.

On the day in question, one of the big trading firms—we'll call them XYZ Commodities—got a *major* opinion on the market. And, although XYZ had been selling all morning, the market was still rising. Seeing this, the pit decided to go along for the ride. Understandably, the locals reasoned that XYZ wouldn't be selling if they thought prices were moving higher.

There's another important factor at work here. That is, trading firms, even enormously successful ones with considerable financial muscle, can change their minds. And that's precisely what happened that day. First, XYZ sold huge quantities in anticipation of lower prices. With the market still rising, however, someone at XYZ decided to take the loss and run. The pit, taking its cue from XYZ's initial bearishness, was still in a selling mood, and that's where John began to get himself in trouble. He took the market personally that day. He had been an early seller and the market rose against him, so he tried to get even by pushing it down single-handedly. When brokers see people bidding into their offers, their egos get involved.

At the time, the market was 55 bid and 60 offered. A second ago, it was 50 bid, 55 offered. That's when John began to offer.

"Sell 100 at 60!" he yelled out into the mob of traders.

"Buy 'em!" yelled XYZ's broker. Now it was obvious that XYZ was changing its mind.

Competing brokers in the pit sometimes don't get along. This was true of John and the XYZ broker, so there was a certain amount of animosity involved in this trade. It was obvious that they were trying to shove the trade down each other's throat. You could hear words exchanged between them. Given the size of the trade, John quickly caught the attention of the pit as this drama began to unfold.

As the market continued to move higher, you could see the adrenaline pass in waves across John's face. He rose his arms in the air, palms outward for selling, and yelled, "Sell a thousand at seventy! A thousand at seventy!"

This must have been exactly what the XYZ broker was looking for because he bought another 700 cars.

After that, the market immediately went to 80 bid on 500, meaning a buyer was willing to pay another two ticks for 500 contracts. The XYZ broker had already made $50 on each of the 700 contracts—a cool $35,000 in seconds. For John, of course, this meant deep trouble.

I knew that John wouldn't be able to extricate himself from this jam. The market went up another 70 points. On the way up, he bought about 300 cars but it was too little too late. Finally, I stopped trading and began to watch his reaction. He turned scarlet red, then sheet white. It wasn't hot in there, but he was sweating. I believe he had the money, but that's not the point. The point is, life is too short to do stuff like that.

Later in the trading session, the market broke a couple of hundred points. But he'd already gotten out. He'd taken a loss on every one of them. A few days later, he sold his exchange membership and retired from the business.

Sometimes you forget how hard this business is on your mind. It is a constant battle of you against yourself. John probably looked in the mirror that night and said: "That's it. I can't take it anymore." It happens even to the best of traders. After a mistake like that, there comes a point where you can't even bring yourself to take a one-lot.

CHAPTER TWENTY-SEVEN _____

_____

What's Ahead— Get Prepared for the Boom and Bust

A favorite saying of mine goes like this: "I'd rather be ten years early than a day late." That's because I suspect that some day the government is going to close down the commodities exchanges because it will need a whipping boy to explain what happened. We've already seen the grain exchanges closed down for a day. That was the first hint of government scapegoating. The possibility of closing the silver market became very real with the Hunts in 1980. The authorities were even talking about shutting down the metals markets for good. The issue finally passed and nothing was done about it. Perhaps because it wasn't the bond or stock market it wasn't considered significant. But the point is clear: *The government will look for a scapegoat when it finds itself in trouble.*

The good news is that the markets will probably flourish as we encounter volatile times ahead. The financials in general should boom as more and more investors learn to use options and futures to manage risk in a volatile market.

UNCERTAINTY ABOUT THE FUTURE

The big swings in volatility have disrupted the "old ways" of doing things and left a lot of people uncertain about the future. This often translates into anger directed at free markets in general. We've already seen the farmers blaming the futures markets for low agricultural prices, and we are going to see more of this trend in the years ahead.

Heightened volatility in the futures markets will certainly prompt the government to conduct "blue-ribbon" investigations and other inquiries. The markets will be blamed for our economic problems because free enterprise has no spokesman. Free enterprise has taken it on the chin from government in the past, and this time it will be no different.

THE WARNING SIGNALS

Before we see any drastic government intervention in the markets, there will be warning signals such as credit controls. In time, however, the government is sure to move against the free markets.

A predictable pattern occurs whenever the government gets involved in "rescuing" a financial institution or "protecting" the public. First, you have a run on the institution's assets followed by government reassurance that there is nothing to worry about. The assurances are a sure sign of trouble.

One thing that's changing is a greater awareness on the part of the public of government's misdeeds in managing the economy. As a result, people have their pulse on government a lot more than they used to. That's because they've been lied to so often in the past. As a result, the market often heats up well in advance of market-moving events being announced.

So what's ahead? We should have several years of high volatility that will be good for the commodities business.

The markets will boom, driven by a pickup in inflation, and speculation will become rampant. But the day of reckoning will come. On that day, you will be trading gold and there won't be a price in dollars anymore. There will be plenty of bids, but no offers. The people with gold will refuse to trade it for dollars. Although I'm not a "hard-money" investor, I think the debt crisis will become that serious.

Now, the country doesn't necessarily have to fall apart before this scenario plays out. There are degrees of crisis. But the implications are serious enough to heed my advice about being ten years early rather than a day late because once the crisis hits, the borders will probably be closed and no money will leave the country. There are frightening implications here that are worth thinking about.

THE ROLE OF UNCERTAINTY

The recent boom in futures and options suggests more and more people, who are tired of undertaking risk, are willing to transfer their risk to someone else. Fortunately, there are plenty of people who are willing to undertake some risk in return for an opportunity to earn a profit. Five years ago it would be hard to find a portfolio manager who would even consider hedging a mutual fund in the S&P market. Today, not to hedge one's portfolio is tantamount to being reckless. The more jittery the world becomes, the more active the options and futures markets will become.

WHAT ABOUT THE REGULATORY AGENCIES?

The Commodity Futures Trading Commission (CFTC) and the National Futures Association (NFA) are regulatory agencies that monitor the markets and the individuals operating in the markets, such as licensed trading advisors and registered brokerage personnel. Unfortunately, these agencies are never there when you need them. Witness the scam operators and schemes we have seen in recent years that neither the NFA nor the CFTC have been able to prevent. It isn't entirely their fault. After all, they are dealing with 50 states that have 50 different sets of rules, some of which are beneficial to the scam artists. Moreover, if somebody wants to cheat someone they will find a way, regardless of how many government agencies there are to police investment practices.

Looking ahead, I think we will see an increase in regulatory activity. To bolster their image, one of these agencies will make an example of some individual—witness the SEC's assault on the insider trading practices—but I'm not optimistic about their overall ability to stem abuses in the marketplace.

THE "PRUDENT" APPROACH

Did you ever wonder why so few people on Wall Street will tell you to buy gold? Perhaps it is because gold is something you store away in a vault for a long time. It isn't something you trade. It doesn't generate commissions.

The main difference between "prudent" money management and "speculative" investing is the amount of time the investment is held. "Prudent" investors lose money over a long period of time by buying Florida real estate in the 1970s or Continental Bank stock at $35 a share. But playing the S&P market or buying gold to stay alive is considered highly speculative.

We may still be in a period when stocks are the only game in town for the prudent investment crowd, but those days are numbered. Economic conditions such as government debt, tax reform and market volatility call for a more comprehensive investment approach.

THE IMPACT OF GOVERNMENT DEBT

There are three things that you can do with government debt: You can pay it off, which is out of the question given today's political situation; you can declare bankruptcy, which no politician in his right mind will ever do; or you can inflate it out of existence. Every politician in recent history has opted for the third approach. So, considering the massive debt with which the government is burdened, we cannot lull ourselves to sleep in assessing economic conditions. We must look to the markets to determine the correct course of action.

You only have to look at the recent rise in metals' prices to see that the markets are sensing a revival in inflation. Everyday, traders in the pit try to explain away why metals are rising, but my instincts tell me that small investors are putting money into gold. They know that the post-Reagan administration probably will be less conservative. Moreover, if gold couldn't break when the price of oil went from $30 to $10 a barrel, what will make it break? Probably nothing. Nevertheless, you won't find the gurus jumping on the gold bandwagon right now; rather, they will wait until it is "safe" to do so—and then, of course, it will be too late.

THE IMPACT OF THE 1986 TAX REFORM ACT

It is still too early to assess the impact of the 1986 tax reform bill, but we can expect to see a greater emphasis on short-term trading. As a result, the stock market is going to become much more like the soybean or sugar markets. Without favorable long-term capital gains tax treatment, there is no incentive to hold onto a security. If a money manager wants to make 20 percent a year and can pick up a quick $5 or $6 profit in IBM or other blue chips, the manager will sell the stock and take the profit. Why not? It makes no difference whether you hold a secu-

rity five minutes or five years. That attitude could provoke
some pretty wicked market moves. We will probably see
fewer sustained bull markets without substantial profit taking. That's going to add even more volatility.

SMALL INVESTORS WILL BE HURT

Heightened volatility will hurt a lot of smaller investors
who aren't prepared for the new market conditions. You
have to look at today's market in terms of your personal
investment approach. If there was ever a market designed
for day trading, this is it. If the name of the game is to
make money, and it no longer matters how the money is
made, the wave of the future is in-and-out trading. The
changes will be considerable, especially in the options
market where you have a high-leverage vehicle in an increasingly volatile environment.

Overall, small inexperienced investors will probably be
hurt by the new investment climate. But from a trading
standpoint, the new investment climate will be the best
ever for day traders and probably the best ever for the
futures market in general. Long-term investors will have to
change their entire orientation if they are going to cope. In
essence, with the passing of the new tax law, the government has said: For four decades we have promoted long-
term investment; now, as a result of this bill, we are
promoting short-term trading. A lot of money managers
already understand that the rules are changing and they
are beginning to act differently.

Already, the brokerage community is in an uproar over
volatility. The brokers in the pit are scared to death. When
a sell order comes into the pit, they offer it down immediately until someone yells, "Buy 'em!" They don't care if
they have to go through two bids to get the order off. That's
how frightened they are of the volatility.

We are also seeing some incredible size traded on stop
orders in this new market. A few months ago, the Dow was

down about 36 points one day and up about 15 or 16 the next. One reason for the rally the next day was that the S&P market ran into some buy stops for about 2,000 contracts. And who do you think sold those contracts? It wasn't the locals. It was the commercials and the arbs who immediately ran to the stock market to buy stocks. And what does that do? It causes the market to rally. An off-floor trader who doesn't see what's going on in the S&P pit may not understand this. But to the pit traders who just saw the commercials and arbs sell the futures, the result is inevitable: *It causes the Dow to jump nine or ten points as the commercials and arbs rush in to purchase stocks.*

THE TAIL WAGS THE DOG

When it comes time for the market to decline, the same scenario is played out in reverse. The market hits sell stops and then plummets. Who do you think was buying? Again, the commercials and the arbs. When they buy futures, they want to lay off the risk if they aren't simply covering their short positions. This, in turn, creates a wholesale rush into the stock market to *sell* stocks. There goes the Dow. When the S&P market causes gyrations in the stock market, it is a case of the tail wagging the dog. That's what has been happening, and it is likely to become common in the years ahead.

The big players are in the market now and the small investor has to take this into account. When you see them coming in—the insurance companies, the mutual funds, pension funds and so on—you can expect the market to become much more volatile. Program trading is just another way for the big players to do what they were going to do originally; but now, with a futures market, they don't have to tip their hands. A large insurance company can come in and sell 2,000 futures to hedge itself without anyone on the Street knowing about it. In the past, they would have had to go into the stock market and sell securities. That, too, would have sent prices lower. The only difference is that now they are going through a middleman, the program trader. Program traders are willing to assume the risk because they can generally lay it off and make a profit.

CHAPTER TWENTY-EIGHT

Mutual Funds and Commodity Pools

The general thinking about stock mutual funds is that given a stable to higher market, you won't be hurt that much and, over time, you may indeed enjoy a profit. It is no secret that mutual funds have been very popular in the recent bull market. The investing public, whether in their retirement investments, such as IRAs or Keogh plans, or as outright investments, have billions of dollars under management in mutual funds. The general thinking, of course, is that mutual funds offer the small investor diversification coupled with so-called professional management.

Commodity pools are similar in concept to mutual funds except that they specialize in futures contracts instead of securities. What's interesting in comparing the two is that one is considered prudent whereas the other is considered speculative. The government, in its infinite wisdom, has deemed the mutual fund safer. In fact, the real difference is that a mutual fund manager can lose all your money over a period of three years, whereas a pool operator will likely speed up the process and lose it in two weeks. In either case, of course, you end up with a loss. But because the mutual fund manager, who might buy auto shares at the top and sell them at the bottom, loses the money over a period of time, he is deemed the prudent investor. Surprisingly, in some quarters, this attitude is acceptable.

Essentially, both mutual funds and commodity pools are run the same way except that the funds can't charge incentive fees. Mutual funds, which are considered "safe" investments because of their emphasis on the securities markets, also tend to raise a lot more money.

ARE THE "PROFESSIONALS" WORTHY OF YOUR MONEY?

The attitude of investors in mutual funds is that they are too busy to watch their own money. That's why they invest in a fund. My attitude is just the opposite. If I'm going to invest in stocks, I'm going to make my own mistakes. I have never seen the so-called "professionals" do well enough in the stock market to give them my money. Moreover, mutual funds are usually loaded with fees.

You have similar problems in the commodity pools. For one, their overall records are not that good. I suspect this is because some people running these pools aren't really professionals. They haven't made their money by trading the market, but by living off commissions and brokerage fees. As a result, many advisors just walk away from a situation when they lose money.

You have to ask some important questions before turning your money over to a commodity pool. What happens if the manager loses the money? What happens to me? What happens to him? The answer to the first question should be obvious, but what about the latter? Does the manager benefit if he loses all the money? If I'm going to lose money, I want the person responsible for the loss *not* to benefit from my misfortune. To draw an analogy, this is like a general leading his troops into battle. If the general stands in back, the troops get shot first. On the other hand, if he truly leads them into battle, he undergoes some risks as well. If I'm a foot soldier, I like to know that the general is up front. So be very careful when you invest in a pool.

HOW TO EVALUATE A TRADING RECORD

Evaluating a manager's trading record is an extremely difficult aspect of investing in a pool. Sometimes it is impossible to make such an evaluation because you can't judge how much risk was at stake. With performance as the key criteria, the impulse is for many managers to simply "roll the dice." If they came up a winner, their record is golden. If they "crap out," however, the investors lose their money. And who's to say one good roll won't be followed by a losing roll? There are so many different ways to alleviate or compound risk that it is difficult to compare two managers. To make an obvious example, it isn't fair to compare the ABC Growth Fund with the XYZ Utility Fund. Everyone knows that utilities can't grow as fast as growth stocks. The same is true of commodity pools. Compare two pools where John Doe, over the past nine months, earned an incredible 900 percent on his money with John Smith who, over the same period of time, earned just 30 percent. Which is better? The obvious answer is the former record of John Doe. But you have to ask yourself if the manager is comfortable with the risk required to reach the 900 percent. The return tomorrow might be zero, or even a negative.

January 23, 1987

Sometimes the lessons of a lifetime are crystallized in a single day. For those of us who trade S&P futures, January 23, 1987, was an unforgettable day. Just as we titled chapter Twenty-eight "The Customers Get Even," we might have titled this postscript "The Gods Get Even." For it certainly seemed like some supernatural forces were at work in the marketplace that day.

THE AFTERMATH OF A NIGHTMARE

Tho professional floor traders who had been selling for weeks into one of the greatest bull markets in history came into the pit that Friday morning in January expecting more of the same—higher prices. Bruised and beaten, most of the pit professionals had become believers, albeit grudgingly. Indeed, by then the pattern had become all too clear: steady to lower on the open and then up—way up. Usually, the locals, many of whom had grown rich fading rallies in more normal times, would short large positions during the day expecting a correction. And sure enough, it would occur. They might get a correction of 50 points, but more often than not, the market would give the short sellers just enough encouragement to provoke tragic trading mistakes.

For example, say that you sell 20 cars at 90, another 20 cars at 65 and a final 20 at 35. You are well situated in a market trading at 15. But you become a bit too self-satisfied, thinking about the nice average price you had on those 60 cars, so you decide to bid 15 on the entire 60. Then what happens? Well, before you had a chance to bid, the brokers would come in bidding the upper 90 on 500 cars and another bid at the upper quarter for 500 and then 65 bid. So you join in the fray and bid alongside of them, and you end up losing a small fortune on what looked so promising just moments before.

That's how it had been all through January. But inveterate short sellers that we are, we locals weren't about to stop selling. I suspect that the first 1,000 point rise in January 1987 was missed by the entire pit. We had just returned from Christmas vacation when it started, and most of us were unprepared for the incredible January run.

To pinpoint the clues to an abnormal market, you have to know the signs of a normal market. When prices are rising day after day in a normal bull market pattern, look for steady to lower prices on the open followed by a rally. We were seeing this pattern day after day, but it wasn't there on January 23, 1987. Instead, the market opened higher and then screamed right through the roof. That was a very important clue. My clients had been badgering me for weeks about this run in the market. Many of them had made sizable profits on their own in the S&P market by simply buying and holding on. It wasn't over yet, they thought, so why not jump aboard? The more the phones rang, the more cautious I became. I knew instinctively that these good times—these unreal times—couldn't persist without severe corrections along the way. In fact, I'd been predicting a sharp break all week. As a veteran gold trader,

I knew all the characteristics of a market top. And sure enough, my phones soon stopped ringing.

EMOTION IN THE PIT

The sentiment in the pit, as we mentioned in previous chapters, can have a profound impact on prices. Often, especially in this bull market, the sentiment has been one-sided. So it wasn't difficult to see that after an initial resistance to higher prices, the pit was tired of selling. They, too, had become bulls and were eagerly waiting to buy that January morning. Just as a horse learns that its rider wants to go in a certain direction after it is hit over the head a few times, the locals realized that it was time to buy.

The bonds opened higher that morning, and so did the S&Ps. That set off some buy programs, and we were off to the races. The locals that morning were about as bullish as I've ever seen them. This one-sided bullishness immediately made me cautious, but I wasn't willing to sell yet. The first couple of times the Dow rallied, I didn't think much of it; it was just normal follow-through. I traded very small numbers for the first few hours. Actually, I was afraid of trading from either side because I knew what was going to happen. "Where's that big break you've been predicting?" the local kept asking. As buyers, they were probably laughing all the way to the bank. Despite the sentiment in the pit, I know it would soon break over 1,000 points and cause a lot of damage.

I wasn't trading for my clients because I was unwilling to lose their money in what I believed would be a certain bloodbath. I was, however, willing to risk a little of my own money. That's different. I started out nibbling on a few long positions. The market went higher, but I was quick to exit the positions because I wasn't comfortable about buying. My primary concern was the end. How—and when—would it come? No one sends out a warning letter before a sharp break. It just happens, and if you are unfortunate enough to get caught, there's no way out. That's why I was trading small from the long side.

Pretty soon, the Dow took off. First, it was up $40, then $45 and even $50. It didn't seem like it wanted to stop. To give you an idea of how bullish the market was, I sold ten cars at a price of 280 even. While I was still carding the trade, it screamed to 281 even. I was out $5,000 in the time it takes to scratch down a few numbers on a piece of paper. No problem. I offer another ten cars and sold them at 281.60. This time, the market rose only 40 points against me, to 282 even, while I was carding the trade. I lost $2,000 on the last ten cars and $10,000 on the original ten.

There comes a point where you have to stanch the bleeding, and we were rapidly approaching that juncture. I decided that I'd buy them all back and take the loss when the market hit 283 even. Meanwhile, I decided to sell another five at 282 even, hoping that would be the top. Unfortunately, the market soon reached 282.50, and I was short a total of 25 cars. Now my selling was starting to attract attention. My trading assistant announced that the Dow was up $62. "Why are you selling?" she asked. I didn't have time to explain what I was doing, but a number of clues were beginning to emerge that made the position look promising.

THE TELLTALE CLUES

First, it was the *wrong time of day* for the market to rally. It was that critical period between 11:00 A.M. and 1:30 P.M. central time. That's when a correction should occur, setting the stage for a rally later in the afternoon. Instead of correcting, however, the market was going crazy. It had opened positive and gone positive. Now was the time for the pullback, but where was it? There was no pullback.

Second, when you have what is known on the floor as the "noon balloon," you have to be careful about buying. As a rule, you can't trust rallies that occur around noon.

The market had been rallying strongly every afternoon that week, so I figured we were overdue for some profit-taking. Then, when we started to get that run at noon, I wondered what would happen by 2:30.

Third, the indicators had turned bearish. The bonds had become noticeably weaker. At first, the market paid no attention to the bonds, but as they continued their downward slide, the signal became harder to ignore. IBM was also in the dumps. How long could the market explode without its price leader?

Lastly, the brokers in the pit were beginning to execute orders that suggested we were in the final throes of a panic. Certain brokers have customers who are pretty good indicators of tops and bottoms. When they came in as buyers of 200 cars at 282.50 (the top proved to be 282.60), I knew it was over. When the brokers who typically fill orders for five, ten or 20 lots came in buying 200 cars at a shot, I knew we had reached the final stage.

Try to understand the psychology at work here. Chances are, the customers had decided to sell. But with higher prices, they simply gave up. They were tired of being short, so in order to recoup their losses they went long in a major way. They planned to ride to the top. Unfortunately, the top was just a couple of ticks away and the bottom was more than 1,000 points away.

7,000 CONTRACTS TO SELL AT THE TOP!

When the pit traders heard the bid to buy 200 cars at 282.50, they responded passionately. I wanted to sell another 20 cars myself, but before I could make my offer a crowd of locals swarmed the broker. "Sold! Sold! Sold!" There was no mistaking their intentions. I later learned that a major brokerage house had placed market orders to sell with about a dozen different brokers. In all, there were 7,000 contracts up for sale.

Anyway, that's how it began. We then had a 500-point

break straight down to 277 even on nothing. I covered quickly on the break, picking up about $20,000 on my 25 cars. So far, we had been experiencing a classic market top, and the drama was far from over. After the sharp break, it began to climb slowly back up. The boulder was being pushed slowly up the cliff for the ultimate tumble. From 277 even, the market rallied back to exactly 280.40, and I knew what was next. This was no random tick. It was the classic pattern I'd been waiting for. I knew that if you were long, this second rally was the time to run. Moreover, if you were thinking of selling, this would be the last opportunity. There wasn't time to ask questions or plot strategies. Surprisingly, a number of floor traders thought it was a bargain. After all, it was their buying that pushed the market up.

I immediately sold 20 cars at 280 even. As I was carding them, the market broke to 278.50. That's when I made a big mistake. I bought them back and made $15,000. If I had kept my mouth shut or covered only half of them, I could easily have had a six-figure day. But I did make $35,000 in two trades, so it wasn't a total loss.

THE FREE-FALL BEGINS

When we went through the previous low at 277, all hell broke lose. There wasn't a buyer anywhere in the pit. You should have heard the offers:

"At half!"

"At even!"

"At half!"

"At even!"

Straight down!

There were no bids. The brokers had unbelievable sell stops. They must have been accumulating for weeks. Every investor in the world wanted to sell the market but there were no buyers. The market broke from 277 down to 266 in a couple of minutes—1,100 points! Down at 266, the S&P

was trading at a 400-point discount to cash, and the Dow had gone from a plus $62 on the day to a minus $55. It was 1:00 P.M.

TOTAL CHAOS

It was hard to believe that the market could continue like that, especially with a 400-point discount, so I decided it was time to buy, so I purchased a six-lot. Why six? I wanted to start with a manageable number, so that if the market moved against me, I could double or triple up.

There were still no buyers. My bid was the first the pit had heard since the beginning of the big break.

"I'll pay even on six cars!" I yelled into the mob.

Immediately, ten guys were all over me.

"I'll sell you 155," said one broker.

"I'll sell you 226," yelled another.

"I'll sell you 85," offered another.

Finally, one broker said, "I'll sell you 225. You pick the price."

I explained that I didn't want to pick the price. I wanted to buy six cars at even.

I'd experienced this so-called "generosity" before: I once bid on ten at a half, and a broker offered to sell me 16 at a half and another five at 45. As soon as I took the trade, he offered 300 at a quarter!

So when this broker wanted to offer me 225 cars at any price, I said I'd buy them at zero.

Between this broker and the others, I could have easily purchased about 500 cars, but my gut instincts told me that if I took them I'd be asking for major trouble. So after beating off their offers, I said, "Well, are you going to sell me those six at even?"

"Sure," he said. "Which even are we talking about?"

Although it was 266 on the board, I agreed to buy them at 267 because that's what I meant when I originally bid. I don't think he cared, though. He probably would have sold them to me at 266.

The confusion was so great at the time that no one really knew where the market was. Indeed, most of the pit had stopped trading altogether to watch us fight over these six cars. Where exactly was the price? Was it 266 or 267? Or perhaps 268? Was that a 280 even offer or a 270 even offer? This general confusion led most traders to put their hands in their pockets. During the few seconds it took to establish that I'd bought at 267 even, the pit grew almost hushed. After the carnage we had just seen, I alone was willing to establish a market by buying six cars at 267.

The plot thickens. As we were carding the trade, the broker behind me bid 274 even on 20 cars. I'd just bought six at 267 even. That's a profit of more than $21,000 in a matter of seconds.

I wasn't about to pass up this opportunity. I turned around and offered to sell him six contracts.

"Take the whole twenty," he said, but I refused.

I sold him the six. Now I was up between $50,000 and $60,000 on the day, so I decided it was time to quit. That last trade could have easily gone the other way.

Despite my good intentions, I wasn't finished yet. The market soon developed a 150-point gap between bid and offer. If the bid were 270.50, the offer was 272.00. That was for the small stuff. If you wanted size, you had to go about 300 either way. After that, I traded seven or eight one-lots and made a couple hundred points on each one—just by making a market and bidding and offering. I was one of the few traders in the pit making a market on one-lots.

About that time, the implications of the carnage we had just witnessed were becoming apparent. Brokerage house officials were wading into the pit in search of traders who had leased seats. They were leading them out of the pit by their sleeves. No brokerage house wanted to deal with the losses and outtrades of leasing members even if they had the $50,000 in earnest money each leasing member is required to post. It was 2:00 P.M. and everyone was in shock.

The final hour was quiet. There was little or no paper. The orders were gone. Many of the locals were destroyed or in a state of shock. The brokers were thinking about their outtrades. It was Super Bowl weekend and many of them were planning to fly out for the big game in Pasadena.

THE AFTERMATH

I'm convinced that if this debacle hadn't occurred on a Friday, the Merc would not have been able to open the next day. As it was, the outtrades clerks worked Saturday and Sunday to resolve many of the trades. One broker's losses amounted to nearly a half million dollars. The outtrade printouts for some brokers looked like a Manhattan telephone directory.

For many of the big brokers, the Super Bowl tickets went unused. For the smaller traders, the realization set in that every trade was nothing more than a $1,000 crap shoot. Take a trade—and bingo!—you win or lose $1,000! That's a game that you aren't going to find too many people to play. Once the market closed, total despair set in. For some, it was the end of a career; for others it was an expensive afternoon. Imagine the amount of money that changed hands: If you did a trade at even and one local thought he was buying at 268 while the broker thought he was selling at 272, the outtrade on a 30 lot would be $60,000. That's an expensive mistake.

HEED THIS ADVICE

If you had followed the advice offered in this book, you would either have caught this move on January 23, 1987, or you would have stayed safely on the sidelines. Chances are, some readers got caught that day. In a sense, these impossible days are not that difficult to foresee. The question is, when will they occur? You have to know the answer if you don't want to get caught on the wrong side of the market.

Since January 23, 1987, the market has been slowly climbing back up. The rock is being shoved to the edge of the cliff again. That means a similar break is almost certain. What's more, the higher the index goes, the worse the correction will be each time. Who's to say the S&P can't break 2,000 or 3,000 points?

One word of advice: If you don't want your stops to be hit, use put options instead of stops for downside protection. Your cost will be the cost of the premium. I know this is a slightly more sophisticated strategy, but stops don't do the job when the market is free-falling. Ask anyone who was filled 1,000 points below the stop price. With puts, you'll make something on those breaks.

Successful trading is an art, not a science. We've tried to provide you with a few yardsticks against which to measure yourself. We hope that you will use them to your advantage. Good luck!

INDEX